# TABLE OF CONTENTS

# FORGE
## (V.) /FORʤ/

to form, especially by concentrated effort; to form or shape an element or object by heating and hammering to mold it into a new shape

Forged is a term used to describe how an object is formed or shaped through diligent and concentrated effort. This concept can be applied to the growing in the Christian faith.

When we trust in Jesus for salvation, He makes us new and begins to mold or shape us more into the image of Jesus. As we grow in our faith, the truth of God's Word shapes our minds and hearts and changes our actions to look more like Jesus.

*You rejoice in this, even though now for a short time, if necessary, you suffer grief in various trials so that the proven character of your faith—more valuable than gold which, though perishable, is refined by fire—may result in praise, glory, and honor at the revelation of Jesus Christ.*

### 1 Peter 1:6-7

# HOW TO USE THIS GUIDE

Hey there!

We are so excited you chose to forge ahead into deeper study of God's Word. As you move toward your teenage years, the Bible can help refine your faith and prepare you to understand and interact with the world around you with a biblical worldview. This preteen discipleship guide will help you on your faith journey of growing in God's Word and living out God's truth.

Follow along with your leader during each session as you read God's Word together and sharpen your knowledge and understanding of who God is and how that changes how you live. Go deeper each week with daily Bible study, prayer, journal pages, key verse memory cards, and opportunities to discuss questions or challenges you might face as a preteen.

Join in the next thirteen weeks as we answer the question "What is truth?" and discuss how to engage those around us with the unchanging truth of the Bible. God is going to use these next few weeks to work in your life to know Him more and evaluate how to live a gospel centered life in your community and world.

—The Forged Team

# WHO DEFINES TRUTH?

Jesus is truth and determines what is true about His creation.

## 🔒 KEY PASSAGE

*John 1:1-18*

## 🗝 KEY VERSE

*John 14:6*

## DEFINE THE WORD

Find a friend and ask him or her to tell you the meaning of these words without looking at them. See if your friend's definitions match up with the correct words.

| suite / sweet | stair / stare |
|---|---|
| some / sum | son / sun |

*Homophones* are words that sound the same but have one intended meaning. This session explores how all truth comes from God, and He alone determines what is true.

# SHARPEN & STRENGTHEN

Truth is found in the person of Jesus Christ. By knowing Jesus and His Word, we can rightly discern what is true so that we may live a life that glorifies Him. As you go throughout your week, use the true words of God to see the world. Ask God to help you evaluate what is truth in your life and reveal any lies you may believe from culture or personal influences. God delights for us to walk in truth, and He will help us!

*What does the Bible say about who defines truth?*

- *Read John 14:6.*
- How does Jesus describe Himself?

- Does Jesus merely say He speaks truth?

*How can we identify cultural falsehoods?*

- What are some beliefs or ideas our culture claims to be true but are really false?

*How does this change how I evaluate what is true in my own life?*

- *Read John 17:17.* Write any notes or thoughts you have about what this means for you.

**Worldview**
How we view the world—our basic beliefs about God, humanity, ethics and the world around us

# FIRE IT UP!

## CHART THE WAY TO TRUTH

Using your Bible, look up the following verses. Fill in the missing words.

1. Psalm 86:11 (CSB): "Teach me your _____,

   LORD, and I will live by your _____. Give me an

   undivided mind to fear your name."

2. Matthew 22:16 (CSB): "Teacher," they said, "we know

   that you are _____ and teach truthfully the

   _____ of God. You don't care what anyone thinks nor

   do you show partiality."

3. 1 John 5:20 (CSB): "And we know that the Son of God

   has come and has given us understanding so that we

   may know the _____ one. We are in the true

   one—that is, in his _____. He is

   the _____ God and eternal life."

4. Psalm 26:3 (CSB): "For your faithful love guides me,

   and I live by your _____."

## TELL ME THE TRUTH

Write down three things about yourself that are true and one thing that is false. Don't show anyone what's not true yet!

1. _____

2. _____

3. _____

4. _____

● Pair up with a friend and see if you can each determine which of the four statements are false. What made it hard to discern the truth from the lie?

_____

_____

_____

_____

_____

**Culture**
The set of shared attitudes, values, goals, and practices that characterizes a group of people

> Jesus is truth and determines what is true about His creation.

# DAILY DISCIPLESHIP

Here are a few tips as you read God's Word and use the journal pages to write down what you learn:

- What does the text say? Write down exact truths from the Bible.
- Let Scripture interpret Scripture. What do these verses mean? Be careful to not insert your own meaning into the text.
- How can you apply the truths of God's Word to your life? How should these truths change the way you think and live?

## DAY ONE

*Jesus is truth.*

- *Read John 1:14; John 3:33; John 18:37; and Psalm 25:5.*

Have you ever heard an idea or fact and wondered if it was really true? Maybe it was something that seemed really extraordinary and hard to believe. With God, we don't have to question what is true because He is truth. Jesus is fully God, and He has all authority and power to determine what is true about His creation. Not only did Jesus create the world and everything in it, but He determined what will be true about His creation. He gave us the right reality by which we should live. Through a relationship with Him, we are able to walk in truth.

- How do the verses provided testify that Jesus is truth?

_____

_____

_____

- How should this change the way you seek after truth?

_____

_____

_____

Sanctify them by the truth; your word is truth.

John 17:17

## DAY TWO

*Truth is knowable.*

● *Read John 1:9,14,16; John 16:13; Psalm 119:30; and John 17:17.*

God has provided us with ways to know truth. First, God has given us His Son so we can know truth. Truth is a person (Jesus), and through a relationship with Him, we can know truth. Secondly, God has given us His Word so we can know what He says is true. God's words always speak truth and provide us with a way to determine what is true about the world around us. God has not left us to figure out truth on our own—He has provided a way for us to know Him!

● How do these verses help us to know truth?

_____

_____

_____

● What or who helps us to know truth?

## DAY THREE

*Truth is absolute.*

● *Read John 1:15-18; Psalm 119:160; Colossians 2:8; and Ephesians 4:20-25.*

Maybe you've had a teacher or a friend who said something that was contradictory to God's Word. You know what they said is false because God's Word gives us what is true. Only God has the authority to declare what is true because He is truth. Not only does He have absolute authority, but who He is never changes. The world might disagree on what is right and wrong or even say it doesn't matter! However, God says that truth is absolute and does not change.

● What do these verses teach about the never changing truth of God?

_____

_____

_____

continued on next page >

● Why is this important for how you make decisions or choices?

## DAY FOUR

*We need the truth for our daily lives.*

● *Read John 1:4-9; Joshua 24:14; Proverbs 8:7; John 3:21; and 1 Corinthians 13:6.*

Have you ever put on a pair of glasses that were the wrong prescription? Or maybe you've swam in a pool and had your eyes burn from the chlorine. If so, you know that it can be hard to see clearly in those situations. If we don't seek to live by God's truth, then our spiritual eyesight is not all that clear either. If truth is important to God, it should be important to us as well. When we live by the truth of God, we live a life that is grounded in all that is right and good. We also glorify God by walking in truth.

● How should we orient our lives around truth in order to live rightly?

● How does your life reflect God's truthfulness?

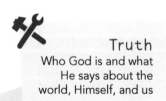

**Truth**
Who God is and what
He says about the
world, Himself, and us

## DAY FIVE

*Truth has eternal significance.*

● *Read John 1:12; Ephesians 1:13; 2 Thessalonians 2:13; and 1 Timothy 2:3-4.*

Knowing truth (Jesus) is the only way to salvation. Different cultures and religions can tell us various beliefs on how we should live and why it matters. What's more, all of these religions or ideas don't agree! Yet God loves us so much that He wants us to know the only true way to Him. Accepting or rejecting the truth of the gospel will have an eternal impact on our lives.

● What eternal impact will knowing and believing truth have on our lives?

_____

_____

_____

● How should you seek to share this truth with others?

_____

_____

## JOURNAL & PRAYER

_____

_____

_____

_____

_____

_____

_____

# WHY SHOULD I TRUST THE BIBLE?

The Bible is the trustworthy Word of God.

## 🔒 KEY PASSAGES

*2 Timothy 3:16-17;*
*Hebrews 1:1-2;*
*Matthew 5:17-18*

## 🔑 KEY VERSE

*Romans 15:4*

## THINK ABOUT IT!

If a tree falls in the forest and no one hears it, did it make a sound? What are some events you know to have happened, but you did not see for yourself?

1. _____

2. _____

3. _____

4. _____

5. _____

# SHARPEN & STRENGTHEN

God's Word is a light unto our feet and guides us on the path of truth. (See Ps. 119:105.) We can trust the Bible because it is the very words of God. Jesus knew the importance of God's Word and used it to teach others about Himself. Scripture is clear that the truth of God's Word is meant to change us. (See Hebrews 4:12.) Will you choose to trust God's Word and turn to it for truth?

### Who wrote the Bible?

- Read 2 Timothy 3:16-17.
- According to these verses, who is the author of the Bible?

### How did we get the Bible?

- Read Hebrews 1:1-2.
- If you had to come up with several explanations to help a friend recognize the Bible as "sacred," what would they be?

### Did Jesus affirm Scripture?

- Read Matthew 5:17-18.
- Find the original reference where Jesus quoted these Scripture verses.
  *Hint: Use a Bible concordance or a cross reference study Bible to help you find the answers.*

Matthew 4:4

_____

Mark 7:10

_____

Luke 19:46

_____

For the word of God is living and effective and sharper than any two-edged sword, penetrating as far as to divide soul, spirit, joints, and marrow; it is a judge of the ideas and thoughts of the heart.

Hebrews 4:12

# FIRE IT UP!

## KEY VERSE CODE-BREAK

Use the key on the right to fill in the consonants that are missing from the verse below, then complete the reference with the circled letters in order. Use the lines at the bottom of the page to write how this truth affects you!

15:4 (CSB)

## WHO WROTE THE BOOK?

Match the author to each book of the Bible by writing a letter in the blank beside each book title. *Hint: Authors can be used more than once.*

**Canon**
The list of all the books that belong in the Bible

A. Ezra
B. Paul
C. John
D. Moses
E. Jeremiah
F. Solomon
G. Luke

____ Genesis
____ Ecclesiastes
____ Lamentations
____ Ezra
____ Revelation
____ Acts
____ 1st and 2nd Corinthians
____ Exodus

## THINK ON IT!

Based on today's Bible study, in your own words, answer the following questions:

● Why can I trust the Bible?

_____

_____

_____

_____

The Bible
is the
trustworthy
Word of God.

● Write down any other ideas or thoughts from today's Bible study that stood out to you.

_____

_____

_____

_____

_____

_____

_____

# DAILY DISCIPLESHIP

Here are a few tips as you read God's Word and use the journal pages to write down what you learn:

- What does the text say? Write down exact truths from the Bible.
- Let Scripture interpret Scripture. What do these verses mean? Be careful to not insert your own meaning into the text.
- How can you apply the truths of God's Word to your life? How should these truths change the way you think and live?

## DAY ONE

*God is the Divine Author of the Bible.*

- *Read 2 Timothy 3:16-17; Galatians 1:11-12; and John 17:17.*

God is the author of Scripture. All truth comes from Him and He has breathed out His words so that we may know Him and what is true. God used men as the vessels by which His words were written, but these men were divinely inspired by God. Since God is truth and the Bible is His Word, the Bible contains all truth. We can trust Scripture to guide us in truth because it is the very words of God.

- Using the space below, write how these verses teach that God is the author of the Bible.

---

---

---

- How can we trust that God is the author of the Bible? Is His Word true?

### Infallible
Free of error; the idea that Scripture is not able to lead us astray in matters of faith and practice

## DAY TWO

*God used men to write down His truthful words.*

- *Read 2 Timothy 3:16-17; 2 Peter 1:20-21; Numbers 12:6-8; and 1 Corinthians 2:12-13.*

What's a favorite book you've read? Most books are great because the author really knows how to tell a good story. However, there is only one Author whose book tells a story that is the source of all truth. Now God, the Author, may have used men to actually write down His words, but these men communicated exactly what God wanted them to. Through the Holy Spirit, God used men like a vessel to write down the words in the Bible and give us a book that helps us to know what is true.

- Did Scripture come from men's own interpretation?

- How did the men speak from God?

## DAY THREE

*God's Word was preserved and is eternal.*

- *Read Hebrews 1:1-2; Psalm 12:6-7; Proverbs 3:5-6; Psalm 119:89; and Matthew 24:35.*

God spoke to Moses and the prophets and later sent His Son to speak truth. These words were kept pure, inerrant, and everlasting. The words are everlasting because God is eternal. God does not change. Therefore, since all truth comes from God, truth does not change. We can't change Scripture to fit our own ideas or beliefs, though some have tried. We must take the Bible for what it says.

**Inerrant**
The truth that Scripture in its original form does not contain anything contrary to fact

continued on next page >

- Can God's Word contain errors? *Circle one.*      Yes      No
- How should we approach reading the Bible when we come to a text that may be hard to understand?

_____

_____

## DAY FOUR

*Jesus believed Scripture is the Word of God.*

- *Read Matthew 5:17-18; Mark 7:9-13; John 8:56-59; Matthew 4:1-11; and Hebrews 4:12.*

Jesus believed the Bible was the authoritative Word of God. He did not question its truthfulness. Jesus taught from the Scriptures. He used the Scripture as the foundation for truth and to reveal the truth to others. He even used Scripture to fight temptation and believed it was able to judge the thoughts of the hearts.

- Did Jesus believe in the historical accuracy of the Bible (example: Noah and the flood)?

_____

- How did Jesus use Scripture against temptation?

_____

_____

## DAY FIVE

*The truth of Scripture points to Jesus.*

- *Read Matthew 5:17-18; Luke 16:17; Matthew 1:22-23; John 3:14-15; John 5:39-36; and Luke 24:27.*

The Bible isn't just a book filled with stories. The Bible is God's revelation to us concerning Jesus. From Genesis to Revelation, all of Scripture points to Jesus. Jesus understood that all of Scripture was written for us to know what is true and to believe in Him. He taught from the Bible concerning Himself so that others would believe. When we read the Bible, we must see that God always intended to point us to the truth about Jesus.

● How do these verses demonstrate that Jesus came to fulfill what was written about Him?

● Why is it important to interpret Scripture with Jesus in mind?

## JOURNAL & PRAYER

**Covenant Relationship**
A mutual agreement between two people or groups of people; The covenant between God and people is unique because God alone sets the conditions.

# WHAT IS TRUE ABOUT GOD?

The Bible tells us what is true about God's nature.

## KEY PASSAGE

*Isaiah 46:3-13*

## KEY VERSE

*Psalm 18:30*

## CAN YOU PICTURE IT?

Draw the face of a famous person and see if a friend can guess who you drew.

What about God? We have not seen the face of God, but God has revealed who He is to us. He has given us His Word so that we may know Him and find truth in Him.

# SHARPEN & STRENGTHEN

God has made Himself known to us through His Son, Jesus, and His Word. God is the one true God who has eternally existed as three Persons of the Trinity. God's attributes tell us what God is like, and we can trust all that God says because He is true. Our God is all-knowing, all-powerful, and is not restricted by any physical boundaries. We can turn to Him for guidance and help, because He knows everything and will always direct us to truth. How can you live differently knowing the truth about who God is this week?

*Who is God?*

● *Read Isaiah 46:9.*

● Who is like God? How would you respond to a friend if they asked you this question?

_____

_____

_____

*What is God like?*

● Write down the following attributes (characteristics) of God as your leader reads them to you.

God is:

_____     _____

_____     _____

_____     _____

_____     _____

*Does God really know everything?*

● Define the word below:

Omniscience: God's complete _____ of _____

and _____ —all past, present and future events, both

actual and possible.

# FIRE IT UP!

## AWESOME ATTRIBUTES

**Attribute of God**
A quality or feature describing the character of God

| | Bible verse: | Attribute: |
|---|---|---|
| 1. | 1 John 3:20 | _____ |
| 2. | Isaiah 6:3 | _____ |
| 3. | Psalm 119:68 | _____ |
| 4. | Deuteronomy 32:4 | _____ |
| 5. | Revelation 1:8 | _____ |
| 6. | 1 John 4:8 | _____ |
| 7. | 2 Corinthians 1:3 | _____ |
| 8. | Romans 2:4 | _____ |
| 9. | Romans 16:27 | _____ |
| 10. | John 17:3 | _____ |

The Bible tells me what is true about God.

This not a complete list, but it is a starting point to learn about what God says He is like. After all, God is infinite, and growing to know Him more and more will be something we can enjoy for eternity! Still, God has revealed Himself to us as a personal God who desires for us to be in relationship with Him. Through Jesus, the image of the invisible God, we have access to knowing God and finding Him to be our all-knowing source of truth.

## A SUPERIOR SAVIOR

My group's superhero is: _____

His/her superpowers are:

_____

_____

_____

How does this superhero fail compared to God?

How is Jesus the superior Savior?

## THEOLOGY ON MISSION

Imagine that you have been tasked by the International Mission Board to teach an indigenous people group about who God is. It is your goal to communicate the attributes you have learned about God to this people group. You can use drawings, a skit, hand motions, or even songs to help this people group understand the God of the Bible. Use the space below to plan out how you will communicate the truth about God.

Doctrine
What the whole
Bible teaches us
today about a
particular topic

# DAILY DISCIPLESHIP

Here are a few tips as you read God's Word and use the journal pages to write down what you learn:

- What does the text say? Write down exact truths from the Bible.
- Let Scripture interpret Scripture. What do these verses mean? Be careful to not insert your own meaning into the text.
- How can you apply the truths of God's Word to your life? How should these truths change the way you think and live?

## DAY ONE

*God is the eternal Creator.*

- *Read Isaiah 46:3-4; Isaiah 45:18; Genesis 14:22; and Romans 1:20.*

Have you ever wondered who made God? If so, the answer is: no one! God is eternal. He is everlasting and He is unchanging. There is no other god like Him. Only He holds the power to create, sustain, and rescue. Yet, lowly as we are, He has revealed Himself to us! We have the joy and privilege to know the living God. God's attributes reveal His divine nature and power so that we can see Him and know His character.

- What does God reveal about Himself in Scripture?

_____

_____

_____

- What does God reveal about Himself through creation?

_____

_____

**Sovereignty**
God's power and control over His creation

_____

_____

_____

## DAY TWO

*There is no one like the all-powerful God.*

● *Read Isaiah 46:5-7; Isaiah 45:5-7; Romans 11:33-34; and Psalm 147:5.*

Many things in the world will try to compete for the place of God. Perhaps there are even idols within your own life which threaten to steal your affections away from the Lord. We were all created to worship, but the question is, *Who* were we made to worship? If you answered God, you are right! Only God is worthy of our worship because only He is the one true God. No worthless idol could ever compare to an all-powerful, all-knowing God who loves us!

● Are there any idols in your life that might be competing for God's rightful place? Remember that idols are not just brazen statues, but anything we put above or in place of God, like pride (self-worship), praise from others, lust for popularity, being an ideal student, and so forth.

● How does knowing God help us to recognize and turn away from such idols?

**Theology**
The study of God and the pursuit of knowing God

## DAY THREE

*God calls us to remember who He is and what He has done.*

● *Read Isaiah 46:8-9; Deuteronomy 5:15; and Psalm 105:5.*

Sometimes we can be a very forgetful people. Even remembering what our parents just reminded us to do can be hard sometimes. As we are easily distracted or busy with life, we can also begin to forget the God of the Bible. We prioritize other things over Him or we fail to stay committed to reading His Word. God knows that we can easily forget that He has done great things for us. There is nothing in our lives that compares to God. We must make it a daily practice to spend time with God and His Word so that our hearts can recall the truths about Him.

continued on next page >

When we remember who God is and what He has done, we are reminded to trust in Him for all things.

● Are there any ways you are easily distracted from remembering the truth of who God is and what He has done?

_____

_____

_____

● What are some ways you can keep track of God's work in your own life and remind yourself to seek Him for all things?

_____

_____

_____

## DAY FOUR

*God is sovereign.*

● *Read Isaiah 46:10-11; Matthew 19:26; Psalm 119:68; Numbers 23:19; and Ezekiel 12:28.*

Sovereign isn't a word we use in our everyday vocabulary. If we lived long ago or in a country with a king or queen, sovereign might be more relevant to us. Essentially, sovereign means "supreme ruler with absolute power." There is no limit to what God can do, and whatever He says He will do, He does. Because God is truth and He is good, all that He does is also true and good. Therefore, we can trust that God rules the world rightly. Additionally, God keeps His promises. His sovereign reign includes the truth that what He has promised will actually be done. He does not leave us with empty promises, but acts sovereignly to fulfill the truth of His Word.

● What do these verses teach about the sovereignty of God?

_____

_____

- How does knowing that God is true and good help you to trust His sovereign rule in your life?

## DAY FIVE

*God is Savior.*

- *Read Isaiah 46:12-13; Psalm 25:5; Ephesians 1:13; and Revelation 19:1-2.*

Have you ever walked around a pitch black room? With no light, you can't see where you are going, and it's easy to trip or run into something. Just finding the light switch can be a challenge. No one wants to wander around in darkness. The Bible teaches us that apart from God, we are in spiritual darkness. Thankfully, God brought the light of His truth to us when He revealed Himself through His Word and His Son, Jesus. Jesus guides us to the truth and helps us to know the God who saves. The true message of the gospel—Jesus' life and teachings—has been given to us that we might be saved. All of God's truth points to Jesus, and by believing in Jesus, we find truth and salvation.

- Have you trusted in the truth of the gospel?

- How has the gospel brought the light of God's truth in to your life? How has this changed the way you live?

> For I am God, and there is no other; I am God and no one is like me.
>
> Isaiah 46:9

# WHAT DOES THE BIBLE SAY ABOUT ME?

The Bible tells us what is true about ourselves.

## 🔒 KEY PASSAGES

*Genesis 1:26-31;*
*Isaiah 43:7;*
*Ephesians 2:1-10*

### 🔑 KEY VERSE

*Psalm 139:14*

## CARBON COPY

Draw a picture in the first box below. Then, ask your friend to copy your drawing in the second box. What do you notice is similar or different?

Your friend's picture is a reflection of your picture, but it isn't an exact match. We were created to reflect the image of our Creator. Today's Bible study helps us to focus on our true identity and purpose in life.

# SHARPEN & STRENGTHEN

Being made in the image of God determines our worth and our purpose. Knowing what is true about who we are and why we were made is foundational to how we view ourselves and how we live. When we trust in Jesus for salvation, God forgives us of our sins and works in our lives to sanctify us (make us more like Jesus). We learn to no longer desire to chase after the false idols we think will fulfill us or define our worth. Instead, we seek to live for Jesus, who took on our sin that we could be made new and righteous. Be encouraged to know how valued you are by God and choose to renew your mind in His truth so that you reflect His glory to the world around you.

### Who does God say I am?

- Read Genesis 1:26-31.
- What is always true about who God says you are?

_____

_____

### What is my purpose?

- Read Isaiah 43:7.
- What are some ways you can glorify God?

_____

_____

_____

**Identity**
Who a person is in relation to what God says is true about them

### Who am I in Christ?

- Read Ephesians 2:1-10
- Listen to your leader and fill in the missing words to the definitions below:

Justification: The truth that when God says that our sins are

_____ , we are _____ _____ .

Sanctification: The _____ of becoming more like

_____ by the power of the _____ _____ .

# FIRE IT UP!

## A NEW CREATION

Read Ephesians 2:10. The word *created* comes from the Greek word *ktizo*, which means "to bring something into existence or to call something into being." In other words, when we are saved by Jesus, we become new creations. Let's do a word study on *ktizo* to see what we as new creations look like as we trust in Jesus.

1. *Read 2 Corinthians 5:17.* What passes away when we become a new creation?

2. *Read Ephesians 4:24.* What is this new creation or new self made like?

3. *Read Colossians 3:10.* How is the new self being renewed?

## THE PERFECT REFLECTION

Sin broke the perfect image of God we originally reflected at the time of creation. Only in Jesus do we see the perfect image of God. Read the verses for each point below and write down how Jesus perfectly reflects God.

*Jesus perfectly reflects what God is like.*
- *Colossians 2:9; Hebrews 1:3; John 14:10; Revelation 1:8*

*Jesus perfectly reflects God's glory.*
- *John 1:14; Titus 2:13; Colossians 1:16; 1 Corinthians 8:6*

*Jesus perfectly reflects God's mission.*

- *1 John 5:20; John 17:3; John 3:16; Philippians 2:10*

_____

_____

_____

## A SECURE IDENTITY

You may have heard the term "identity crisis." This occurs when people have gone through or are going through a time of change that causes them to question who they are and what they are called to do. Straight A's become C's, a relationship fails, a sports injury occurs—whatever the circumstance may be—these changes cause some to question their identity. However, God declares that our identities are secure in Him. Regardless of an earthly circumstance, God says we are valued and loved by Him. He gives us our identity and purpose.

**Sin**
To think, say, or behave in any way that goes against God and His commands

- Are there any areas of your life that you may be tempted to place your identity in?

_____

_____

- *Read Ephesians 2:1-10.*
- How do these verses give us confidence to find our identity in who God says we are?

_____

The Bible tells me what is true about me.

For we are his workmanship, created in Christ Jesus for good works, which God prepared ahead of time for us to do. **Ephesians 2:10**

# DAILY DISCIPLESHIP

Here are a few tips as you read God's Word and use the journal pages to write down what you learn:

- What does the text say? Write down exact truths from the Bible.
- Let Scripture interpret Scripture. What do these verses mean? Be careful to not insert your own meaning into the text.
- How can you apply the truths of God's Word to your life? How should these truths change the way you think and live?

## DAY ONE

*We are made to reflect God.*

- *Read Genesis 1:26-31 and 1 Corinthians 11:7.*

Man and woman were made to reflect God. We know that God is Spirit, so we don't physically look like God, but we can show God to the world by our unique talents, our creativity, our love towards our neighbors, using our minds for good, speaking truth, and so on. Being made in God's image also sets us apart from the rest of creation. No other created thing bears the image of God—only humanity. Think of a mirror that has a light shining on it. When the light hits, it reflects outward. Bearing God's image is the same way. We shine God's nature into the world around us just by being made in His image.

- Are you seeking to reflect God to the world?

- Why is being made in God's image such an important truth to believe?

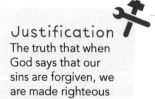

Justification
The truth that when God says that our sins are forgiven, we are made righteous

## DAY TWO

*All people are valued and equal.*

● *Read Genesis 1:26-31; James 3:9; and Luke 12:6-7.*

Sanctification
The process of becoming more like Jesus by the power of the Holy Spirit

All people are made in the image of God. Every race, every culture, unborn and born were created by God to bear His image. Yet, in our sin, we speak unkindly toward our neighbor. In our pride, we think we are superior to others. Sometimes our hearts fail to recognize that the lonely kid at school was specially made by God and for God. No one is better or worse than the other. We are equal in the sight of God, and we should view each other the same way. Likewise, we are all valued by God. Our value comes from being made in His image, not by our achievements or appearance or popularity. We find our value in the truth that God loves us so much and that He specifically made us to reflect Him.

● How should this truth change how we act toward and view other people?

● Does God approve of our behavior when we diminish the image they bear with unkind words or actions?

## DAY THREE

*We are made for His glory.*

● *Read Isaiah 43:7; Matthew 5:16; 1 Corinthians 10:31; and Revelation 4:11.*

Most people want to live a life of purpose. No one wants to look back over their life and be filled with regret or feel as though their life did not count for much. When God created us, He invited us to be a part of the greatest purpose of all—glorifying Him. It is what we were made to do, what our hearts long for, and what brings ultimate joy. We all have a choice whether or not we will join God in this holy purpose. C.S. Lewis said, "For you will certainly carry out God's purpose, however you act, but it makes a difference to you whether you serve like Judas or like John."[1] God doesn't force us to be on mission with Him, but He

continued on next page >

does want to guide us to the true nature of our created purpose. In this mission we find our greatest joy.

- How will you respond to God's created purpose for you?

- Will you seek to glorify Him in all things? Or will you choose to live for yourself?

## DAY FOUR

*Sin broke our perfect reflection.*

- *Read Ephesians 2:1-10; Genesis 3:17-19; and Isaiah 53:6.*

God created people to perfectly reflect Him, yet because of sin, that image is broken. We are still able to reflect who God is, but sin has distorted the picture. Not only do we not see ourselves rightly, but we fail to see God rightly as well. Sin not only tarnished the image, but it brought death and destruction to the world. Rather than live according to God's truth, we went astray and chose to live by our own fleshly desires.

- How have you seen sin distort the image we are to reflect?

- In what ways do we, as broken people, live for ourselves rather than desire to reflect God to the world?

## DAY FIVE

*Jesus redeems our broken image.*

- *Read Ephesians 2:1-10; Romans 8:29; 2 Corinthians 3:18; and Colossians 3:10.*

God is faithful, and He keeps His promises. Soon after sin came into the world, God made a promise that He would defeat sin and death. He promised to restore what sin had destroyed, including the broken image we bear. Jesus is the perfect image of God. Being fully man and fully God, only He could redeem what was broken. By faith in Jesus, we are being renewed day by day as God conforms us into the image of His Son. As we seek to have our minds renewed by truth, we are better able to walk in light of His saving grace and become more like Jesus.

- Using the passages above, how are you being transformed into the image of Jesus?

- What are some ways you can look to Jesus everyday in your own life?

## JOURNAL & PRAYER

# WHAT DOES THE BIBLE SAY ABOUT THE CHURCH?

The Bible tells us what is true about the church.

## 🔒 KEY PASSAGES

*Ephesians 2:11-22;*
*Acts 2:42-47;*
*Ephesians 4:11-16*

## 🔑 KEY VERSE

*Hebrews 10:23*

## GET DOWN TO IT!

Starting with the word below, change or delete one letter to find a four-letter word with no "i."

| | | | | | |
|---|---|---|---|---|---|
| S | T | E | A | K | a large piece of meat |
| ⬇ | ⬇ | ⬇ | ⬇ | ⬇ | to say something out loud |
| ⬇ | ⬇ | ⬇ | ⬇ | ⬇ | the top a mountain |
| ⬇ | ⬇ | ⬇ | ⬇ | ⬇ | a fruit sort of like an apple |
| ⬇ | ⬇ | ⬇ | ⬇ | | to rip |
| ⬇ | ⬇ | ⬇ | ⬇ | | one way to describe the church |

# SHARPEN & STRENGTHEN

The church is a group of believers who meet together to worship and serve God. Members of a church have professed faith in Jesus and desire to live according to His Word. Church is a place for believers to grow in their faith through studying right teaching, living out our faith, building up one another, encouraging each other, worshiping God, and telling unbelievers about Jesus. The church's primary goal is to glorify God. Are you part of a local church? If so, how do you participate as an active part of your church? If not, how can you pray and seek God's wisdom as you consider what it means to be part of a local church?

### Who is the church?

● *Read Ephesians 2:11-22.*

● Can you go to church but not really be a part of God's family of believers? Explain.

_____

_____

_____

**Church**
A group of believers who meet together to worship and serve God

### What is the purpose of the church?

● *Read Acts 2:42-47.*

● What actions do we participate in within the church that bring God glory?

_____

_____

### Why go to church?

● *Read Ephesians 4:11-16.*

● What did Paul say in these verses that could happen if we choose not to gather together for worship regularly?

_____

_____

_____

continued on next page >

● What are the positives to being a part of the body of Christ?

# FIRE IT UP!

## HE IS FAITHFUL

*"Let us hold on to the confession of our hope without wavering, since he who promised is faithful." Hebrews 10:23*

Draw a picture of how you might use this key verse in your own life. When is a time that this verse would be helpful to remember?

## BAPTISM & THE LORD'S SUPPER

If you've been a part of a church for a while, you have probably witnessed someone being baptized and seen people participate in the Lord's Supper. These are what we call ordinances, or commands, given by Jesus to perform. We participate in these ordinances within a local church for specific reasons. Using the Bible references, answer the following questions to understand more about the purposes of these ordinances and why they are important.

The Bible tells me what is true about the church.

1. *Read Matthew 28:20.* Who commanded us to baptize?

2. *Read Romans 6:4-5.* Baptism does not save us. It is a symbol. What does it symbolize?

3. *Read Matthew 26:26-29.* Who commanded us to take the Lord's Supper?

4. *Read 1 Corinthians 11:23-26.* Why do we take the Lord's Supper? What does it symbolize?

5. *Read 1 Corinthians 10:16-17.* Who does Paul say should participate in the Lord's Supper?

## ONE ANOTHER PASSAGES

Using a Bible concordance or Bible app, look up the phrase "one another" in the New Testament. Read 5-7 of these different passages and record the references below. Then write a brief summary of how these passages teach what relationships in the church should look like.

Regenerate
Born again, a new creation; spiritually speaking, this term reflects what happens when a person becomes a Christian

# DAILY DISCIPLESHIP

Here are a few tips as you read God's Word and use the journal pages to write down what you learn:

- What does the text say? Write down exact truths from the Bible.
- Let Scripture interpret Scripture. What do these verses mean? Be careful to not insert your own meaning into the text.
- How can you apply the truths of God's Word to your life? How should these truths change the way you think and live?

## DAY ONE

*We are one in Jesus.*

- *Read 1 John 1:8-9; Ephesians 2:9-22; and 1 Corinthians 12:13.*

How would you define sin? The Bible teaches us that sin means to miss the mark—to think, say, or behave in any way that goes against God and His commands. Romans 3:23 teaches us that everyone has sinned. We all choose to disobey God and our sin deserves God's punishment of death. The good news is that God didn't leave us in our sin. God sent Jesus—the perfect solution to our sin problem—to rescue us from the punishment we deserve. Jesus alone saves us. Because Jesus gave up His life for us, we can be welcomed into God's family for eternity! Everyone who trusts in Jesus becomes one in Him. We should choose to belong to a local body of believers who are also a part of His family.

- How do these verses teach that Christians are a part of God's family?

_____

_____

_____

- Does it make a difference who we are or where we come from? Explain.

_____

**Reconciled**
The removal of iniquity (sin) and restoration between God and people

_____

_____

_____

## DAY TWO

*We are united as the body of Christ.*

- *Read Ephesians 2:11-22; Galatians 3:28-29; Colossians 3:14-15; and Romans 7:4.*

Have you ever had an argument with a friend before—maybe even a best friend? Arguments and disagreements can cause division. They can lead us to not be as close as we were to our friends, or we can find it hard to forgive and repair the friendship. In Jesus, we are called to live in unity with others. We are to lay aside our differences of opinion or disagreements with other Christians and be united in our faith. Through our hope in the gospel, we are united to one body and belong to one another. Being unified in our faith helps us to do the work God has called us to do.

- Is any one person better than the other within the church? Why or why not?

- What should we "put on" in order to remain in unity with others?

## DAY THREE

*We are being built into a spiritual house for God.*

- *Read Ephesians 2:20-22; 1 Peter 2:4-9; and Ephesians 4:15-16.*

Some houses are made of bricks or stones. Each brick fits perfectly together to form the house. In order for the house to stand firm, it must first have a strong foundation. While the church is not a building, the Bible does call the people of God "living stones." We are living through new life in Christ and being built into a spiritual house for God to dwell. Jesus is our strong foundation. Through our faith in Christ, we are united into a spiritual house which God is able to use for His glory.

continued on next page >

● How does God build His spiritual house?

_____

_____

_____

● What are we to offer or do as the people of God?

_____

_____

_____

## DAY FOUR

*We are called to be a living church.*

● *Read Acts 2:42-47; 1 Timothy 3:15; 1 Corinthians 14:26; Hebrews 10:25; and Matthew 28:19-20.*

The church is meant to be a living structure because it is made of people who have been given new life through Jesus. God's ultimate purpose for the church is to bring Him glory, but the church can bring glory to God in many ways. Just going "to church" doesn't mean we are living out God's mission. We are called to not only know true teaching but to also live out that teaching in our everyday lives. The Bible gives us clear instruction for how we should live as the church, work together, and be unified in the commands given to us in Scripture.

● What are different ways we can live as the church to glorify God?

_____

_____

_____

● How can we encourage one another to live in a way that pleases God?

_____

_____

_____

## DAY FIVE

*We mature in faith as we grow to be more like Jesus.*

- *Read Ephesians 4:11-16; Romans 12:5-6; Colossians 1:9-10; Colossians 2:6-7; and Ephesians 4:32.*

We often measure growth by height. When you visit the doctor for a checkup, the nurse measures your height. Maybe you've planted seeds and watched them grow into tall sturdy plants. In the church, spiritual growth is measured differently. It is measured individually, but also as a whole. Both as individuals and as a whole, we grow by how we mature in our faith. Are we becoming more and more like Jesus? Being a part of a community of believers helps us to grow in our faith. God did not create us to live in isolation. He wants us to grow together!

- What are ways we can grow to be more like Jesus?

- How can you, with your local church, grow to walk in a manner worthy of the Lord?

- What does it mean to do all things for "building up"?

## JOURNAL & PRAYER

# WHAT IS THE BIBLE ALL ABOUT?

The Bible is God's message about Himself and His salvation plan through Jesus.

## 🔒 KEY PASSAGES

*Genesis 1:31*
*Genesis 3;*
*Genesis 3:15*
*Romans 3:21-26;*
*Acts 3:19-21*

## 🔑 KEY VERSE

*Romans 3:23-24*

## STORY IN A STORY

What is one of your favorite stories?

What part of the story do you love best?

What do you love this story? Why is it so special to you?

# SHARPEN & STRENGTHEN

Stories are powerful tools that can sometimes share truths, morals, or actions that appeal to our imaginations. These stories invite us to imagine what it might look like if we were a part of them. The Bible is one big story, and God is telling us the story of what He is doing, and inviting us to become a part of it. The Bible is God's message about Himself and His salvation plan through Jesus.

### *Where does the story start?*

- *Read Genesis 1:31.*
- What did God say about everything He had made?

- How do you think God's creation looked then that is different from today?

### *What has God done in the story?*

- *Read Genesis 6:6.*
- Noah and his family are one part of the story of redemption. How does the story of Noah point toward a greater rescue? Explain.

- What Bible stories can you think of that show God saving His people?

**Restoration**
The truth that God is making all things new

### *Where is the story headed?*

- *Read Acts 3:19-21 and Revelation 21:1-5.*
- God's story isn't finished. He has done great things, but He is still working to make all things new. We call this restoration.

# FIRE IT UP!

## WRITE THE STORY

Review the four parts of the biblical narrative (creation, fall, redemption, restoration) by reading the Bible verses below. Then write a summary of God's story in your own words.

- *Genesis 1:1-2; 1:27; Romans 3:23; Ecclesiastes 7:20; Ephesians 1:17; Mark 10:45; Titus 2:14; Acts 3:21; Romans 8:21; 1 Corinthians 15:26*

**The fall**
The coming of sin
into the world

## SEEING JESUS THROUGHOUT THE BIBLE

The story of the Bible centers around Jesus. Jesus made His entrance into the world long after the Old Testament had been written. However, the stories of the Old Testament all point to Jesus. He is the greater Moses, the superior Joseph, and the perfect King David. In Luke 24:27, Jesus says that all the Scriptures point to Him. Reading the Bible verses on the next page will help show how Jesus is at the center of every story.

Match the Bible references to the correct story.

____ Jesus is the better Adam.

____ Jesus is the better sacrifice.

____ Jesus is the better Moses.

____ Jesus is the better Jonah.

____ Jesus is the better prophet, priest, and king.

a.  Deut. 8:15, 1 John 2:1, Acts 5:31

b.  Jonah 2:1-10, Mark 4:35-41

c.  1 Corinthians 15:21-23

d.  Genesis 22:7-8, 12-14

e.  Exodus 33:7-23, 1 Timothy 2:5-6

## GOD IS WRITING YOUR STORY

God has given us the Bible so that we may know Him and know what is true. He wrote His story so that we could be a part of it through Jesus. Hebrews 12:2 tells us that Jesus is the author and perfecter of our faith. He is working to finish our story that we may finish the race well.

● How have you seen God work in your life (story) so far?

_____

_____

_____

**Redemption**
God's work to release believers from the consequences of sin when they trust in Jesus

● What hope do you have knowing Jesus is faithful and will finish the work He has began?

_____

_____

_____

The Bible tells me what God has done and what he is doing.

_____

_____

_____

_____

_____

# DAILY DISCIPLESHIP

Here are a few tips as you read God's Word and use the journal pages to write down what you learn:

- What does the text say? Write down exact truths from the Bible.
- Let Scripture interpret Scripture. What do these verses mean? Be careful to not insert your own meaning into the text.
- How can you apply the truths of God's Word to your life? How should these truths change the way you think and live?

## DAY ONE

*The story begins with the creation of the world.*

- *Read Genesis 1:31; Genesis 2:3; John 1:1-3; Romans 1:20; and Romans 11:36.*

The Bible is not some fairy tale. We've heard the "once upon a time" stories with made-up heroes and wicked villains. These stories may help us learn about good and evil, but they do not tell us all we need to know. The Bible is a book filled with true stories that tell us who God is, what He has done, and what He will do. The Bible takes us back to the very beginning before any story ever existed. Nothing existed before, except God Himself. God is the Author of the story, and He began His work before creation. The Bible tells us what is true about God and the story He is writing.

- What do these verses teach about the beginning of God's story?

_____

_____

_____

- Why did God create the world?

_____

_____

_____

_____

## DAY TWO

*The story experiences ruin through sin.*

- *Read Genesis 3; Romans 5:12; Isaiah 53:6; Romans 3:23; Romans 6:23; and Galatians 5:19-20.*

Have you ever created something only to have it ruined or destroyed? Maybe you painted a picture and accidentally spilled something on it. Or maybe you built an awesome creation from blocks, but your little sibling knocked it down. In a similar way, this is what happened to God's story. God made a beautiful and perfect creation, but man ruined it through disobedience. Rather than submit to the Author of the story, we wanted to be the author ourselves. Sin entered the world when Adam and Eve chose the fruit over their love for God. Now all of creation suffers the consequences of sin.

- What are the consequences of sin?

- How has sin corrupted our own hearts?

## DAY THREE

*The story is redeemed through a Savior.*

- *Read Genesis 3:15 and Romans 3:21-26; Titus 2:14; Galatians 3:13; 1 Peter 1:18-19; and Revelation 5:9.*

Most stories have a hero. In comic books, we see heroes who wear capes and have extraordinary powers. In fairy tales, we read of princes who rescue someone in need, or princesses who save their people. A story is made great by the actions of the hero, because we all want an ending where good triumphs over evil. God provided us with the greatest Hero who ever existed—Jesus. God's story doesn't end with death and destruction. Through the life, death, and resurrection of Jesus, God redeemed what sin corrupted. Jesus was promised immediately after

continued on next page >

God cursed the earth because of sin. God always had a plan to redeem what sin had broken.

● How are we redeemed through Jesus?

_____

_____

## Atonement
The work of Jesus to cover or cancel sin; Jesus made atonement for our sins when He died on the cross

● Who does/will Jesus ransom for God?

_____

## DAY FOUR

*The story will be restored with Jesus' return.*

● *Read Acts 3:19-21 and Revelation 21:1-5; Romans 8:19-21; Joel 2:25-26; and 2 Corinthians 4:17.*

It's hard to picture what earth will look like with no sin. We all experience sin's consequences in our lives. We hurt others and others hurt us. There is a degree of suffering in everyone's lives, but we can remember that Jesus conquered the grave. Because of Jesus' resurrection we have hope, but that hope has not revealed itself fully. We see with eyes of faith, believing that God will one day restore all things. God has promised that Jesus will return, and when He does, there will be a new heaven and a new earth. Sin and death will be defeated once and for all. All things will be made new. Jesus will reign and His kingdom will know no end— our joy will be eternal as we dwell with Him.

● Who first spoke of God restoring all things?

_____

● What will happen to the first earth and heaven?

_____

_____

_____

_____

- How will our suffering be restored?

## DAY FIVE

*Jesus is the Author and Perfecter of our faith.*

- *Read Revelation 21:1-5; Hebrews 12:1-2; Ephesians 4:21-22; Galatians 6:7-10; and 1 Thessalonians 5:24.*

Did you know that Jesus is the Author of your story? It's true! If you have placed faith in Jesus, then He has joined your story to His story of redemption and restoration. Sin brought us death, but Jesus gave us life! Jesus began a work in us when He sealed us with His redeeming blood. He will finish the work He began; however, we are still to live by faith as we run the race Jesus has set before us. Running a race can be tiring, but if we look to Jesus, we will find the strength and the grace to run with endurance.

- Jesus will one day finish our story, but what responsibility do we have as we live by faith?

- What does "we reap what we sow" mean?

- How do we "sow to the Spirit"?

# IS THE BIBLE MORE IMPORTANT THAN OTHER BOOKS?

The Bible is holy and different than sacred texts of other religions and worldviews.

## 🔒 KEY PASSAGE

1 Corinthians 15:1-11

## 🗝 KEY VERSE

2 Timothy 3:16-17

## I BELIEVE IT!

Have you or one of your friends ever believed that something was true only to find out you were wrong? *(Example: What if you believed yogurt was actually pronounced yo-GRIT?)*

● How did you learn what was really true?

_____

_____

_____

_____

_____

# SHARPEN & STRENGTHEN

The Bible is the only book in the world that contains the holy words of God. The Bible's trustworthiness is proven by the prophecies that came true, the thousands of inerrant copies spanning thousands of years, eyewitness testimonies, and transformed lives. Every other religion or worldview doesn't come close to the Bible's truthfulness. If we believe that the Bible is God's Word, then it must become the most important book in our lives.

*How is the Bible different from other books?*

- *Read 1 Corinthians 15:1-4.*

- Decode the message by cracking the code! *Hint: replace each letter with the letter that comes before it in the alphabet.*

In the Christian faith, our beliefs are _ _ _ _ _ _ _ _ _ _ to the
               B O D I P S F E

_ _ _ _ _ _ _ _ _ _ _ _ _ of Jesus.
   S F T V S S F D U J P O

*What other evidence proves the Bible is true?*

- *Read 1 Corinthians 15:5-7.*

- What is a witness or eyewitness testimony?

_____

_____

*What makes the Bible holy and special?*

- *Read 1 Corinthians 15: 8-11.*

- How has the Bible changed your life?

## Eyewitness Testimony

Witness to an event, someone who has seen something with their own eyes and shares their experience

# FIRE IT UP!

## THE UNITY OF THE BIBLE

Did you know that the Bible was written by over 40 different authors spanning 1500 years? Even with that many authors from different time periods, the Bible contains one unified message. Jesus is the central figure of the Bible from Genesis to Revelation.

● Follow the instructions from your leader to complete this activity.

## Worldview
How we view the world—our basic beliefs about God, humanity, ethics, the world around us

## MIRRORED MANUSCRIPTS

Remember that the Bible was written down by scribes. Every scribe copied books or portions of Scripture to be preserved and passed onto future generations. With a partner, you will practice copying a Bible verse. One partner will see the verse and begin writing it down, while the other "scribe" will copy down the verse as it is being written. Both partners should end up with the exact same verse.

The Bible
is holy and
different
than sacred
texts of
other
religions and
worldviews.

## THE BIBLE & CHANGED LIVES

- Read 1 Thessalonians 1:6-10.
- How did the Word of God change the lives of those in the church at Thessalonica?

- What did they do with the Word of God?

# DAILY DISCIPLESHIP

Here are a few tips as you read God's Word and use the journal pages to write down what you learn:

- What does the text say? Write down exact truths from the Bible.
- Let Scripture interpret Scripture. What do these verses mean? Be careful to not insert your own meaning into the text.
- How can you apply the truths of God's Word to your life? How should these truths change the way you think and live?

## DAY ONE

*The resurrection is key to redemption.*

- *Read 1 Corinthians 15:1-4; 1 Corinthians 15:12-19; Romans 1:4; and Acts 4:12.*

The biblical story of redemption is centered on the resurrection of Jesus Christ. Without the resurrection, our faith if futile. The fact that the resurrection did occur confirms the authority and truthfulness of God's Word. Jesus died and was raised from the dead three days later. Most religions are founded on a works-based salvation—believing you can earn a right relationship with God through right actions. Only the gospel of Jesus Christ reveals that we could never save ourselves—we could never be good enough on our own. Only faith in Jesus will redeem us from our sin. Over and over again, the Bible refers to the Christian's faith being connected to the resurrection of Jesus.

- Why would our faith be useless if Jesus was not raised from the dead?

_____

_____

- How did the resurrection prove that all the words that Jesus claimed about Himself were true?

_____

_____

_____

_____

## DAY TWO

*The Old Testament prophecies were fulfilled.*

- *Read 1 Corinthians 15:1-4; Micah 5:2; Daniel 2:44; Isaiah 53:1-7; Zechariah 9:9; and Psalm 16:10.*

Have you ever made a guess about something that could happen—maybe when a baby would be born or what the final score of a game might be? It can be fun to make predictions and see if we'll be right. However, our guesses are just guesses because we don't have the power to make them come true. On the other hand, the Bible has correctly predicted future events. Some Bible scholars say there are over 300 fulfilled prophecies about Jesus. The probability of this number of prophecies coming true from sheer coincidence is mathematically almost impossible. However, a book written by an all-knowing, all-powerful God could easily predict future events with ease. No other religion or person could tell what will happen in the future. Only a special book like the Bible can do that. The verses above are just a few of the prophecies about Jesus.

- How were these verses fulfilled in Jesus?

- How do these fulfilled prophecies help us to truly believe the Bible is the most important book?

## DAY THREE

*There were many witnesses to the resurrection.*

- *Read 1 Corinthians 15:5-7; Acts 2:31-32; Luke 1:2-3; 2 Peter 1:16; and Acts 1:1-3.*

In our court system, we use credible eyewitness testimonies to prove innocence or guilt. A jury cannot give a verdict without proof from the witnesses of others. The more witnesses there are, the stronger the

continued on next page >

testimony. The resurrection of Jesus had more witnesses than needed to prove it really happened. Even the life, miracles, and death of Jesus had countless witnesses. These eyewitnesses testified truthfully to the events in the Bible, and they were willing to die for what they believed. Many were martyred for the sake of the gospel.

● Think about all of the people who Jesus appeared to after His resurrection. How do these eyewitness accounts give you confidence that God's Word is true?

## DAY FOUR

*Paul's life was changed through Jesus.*

● *Read 1 Corinthians 15:8-11; Hebrews 4:12; 1 Peter 1:23; John 7:38; and John 17:8.*

God's story of salvation is found all throughout the Bible, from the nation of Israel to individual people like Rahab and Ruth. When God saves someone, their lives are changed forever. The apostle Paul was no exception. Before his encounter with Jesus, Paul was a zealous, religious man who ruthlessly persecuted Christians. He hated all things related to Jesus...but then He met Jesus and everything changed. The testimony of a changed life is a powerful witness. In the Bible, we find the words that lead us to a new life full of hope, joy, and peace. The Bible is a book unlike any other because it contains living words.

● How do these verses show that God's Word is powerful?

● Why does this make the Bible different from other books?

## DAY FIVE

*Paul preached the Word of God.*

● *Read 1 Corinthians 15:1-11; 2 Timothy 4:1-5; Romans 1:16; and Ephesians 1:13.*

Twice in 1 Corinthians 15, Paul says that he preached the Word of God. In both of these cases, the preaching of the Word led to salvation. The Bible is a book that we read individually, but it is also a book that is to be proclaimed to people everywhere. We should never be ashamed to proclaim the Word of God to those we know or even those we don't know. God's Word leads people to salvation, and therefore it is a book that is to be shared. God's Word will not return void. It will fulfill the purpose God has for it. Unlike other religious texts or worldviews, the Bible will always guide us in truth and toward Jesus.

● What consequences come from not preaching the Word or knowing our Bible?

_____

_____

● How will you share God's Word with others?

_____

_____

## JOURNAL & PRAYER

_____

_____

_____

_____

There is no other name under heaven given to people by which we must be saved.

### Isaiah 46:9

# WHY SHOULD I CARE ABOUT WHAT THE BIBLE SAYS?

The Bible leads us to walk in a manner pleasing to God.

## 🔒 KEY PASSAGE

*Ephesians 4:17-32*

## 🗝 KEY VERSE

*Matthew 4:4*

## SEED TO TREE

How does a seed become a fully grown tree? What does it need to grow? Draw what you imagine a seed looks like in four different stages of growth.

1.

2.

3.

4.

# SHARPEN & STRENGTHEN

The Bible is the most important book we will ever read. By the truth found in the Bible, we grow in our relationship with Jesus and are able to have our minds renewed according to what is good and true. A renewed mind helps us to live as the new creation we are made into when we trust in Jesus as our Savior. By reading God's Word, we are made more and more into the image of Jesus. God is glorified by our desire to want to know Him more and look more like Jesus. Be encouraged to read God's Word every day, and God will be faithful to your obedience.

*How does the Bible grow our relationship with God?*

- Read *Ephesians 4:17-21.*
- Decode the message by cracking the code! *Hint: Replace each number with it's matching letter in the alphabet.*

We should __ __ __ __ what the __ __ __ __ __ says because it
        3  1 18  5             2  9  2 12  5

__ __ __ __ __ us __ __ __ __ __ __ __ __ to be __ __ __ __ __ __ in
8  5 12 16 19      3 15 14 20  9 14 21  5       18 15 15 20  5  4

__ __ __ __ __ .
10  5 19 21 19

- Who first taught you God's Word? Do you have a favorite Bible verse? Write it below and explain why it is your favorite.

_____

_____

_____

*How does the Bible renew our minds?*

- Read *Ephesians 4:22-24.*
- What kind of change happens to a caterpillar?

It __ __ __ __ __ __ __ a __ __ __ __ __ __ __ __ __ __ !
   2  5  3 15 13  5 19     2 21 20 20  5 18  6 12 25

- God tells us to renew our minds because correct thinking and belief leads to right living by faith.

continued on next page >

*What does the new self look like?*

- *Read Ephesians 4:24-32.*
- This side of heaven, we will never be totally sinless. However, God is working in us to transform us more into the image of Jesus. We call this process *sanctification.*

# FIRE IT UP!

## A LIFE PLEASING TO GOD

Becoming a follower of Jesus makes us into a new creation. God begins the process of transforming us into the image of Jesus. The Bible helps us to know Jesus so that we can renew our minds and live like Him. Look up the following verses and answer each question.

1. *Read Psalm 1:1-3.* What is the delight of the person who loves God?

2. *Read Romans 12:1-2.* How are we able to know God's will?

3. *Read Colossians 1:10-12.* What does a transformed life look like?

4. *Read Galatians 5:22-24.* What is the fruit of a life transformed by the gospel?

Renewed
Completely
transformed

## QUEST FOR MEANING

Reading our Bibles transforms us more into the image of Jesus, but sometimes understanding what a specific verse or passage in the Bible means can be difficult. Studying the Bible is meant to tell us what God says, not what we say or want the text to mean. One of the best ways to study the Bible is to ask questions about the verse or verses you are reading. Try asking a question about what a word means or how this verse connects to another verse in the chapter. Maybe you ask a question about where else the Bible mentions a specific word or phrase. By studying the Bible this way, we get to the real meaning of what God says. Check out "How Do I Study My Bible" on page 110 to learn more!

> The Bible leads us to walk in a manner pleasing to God.

*Let's try it out...*

- *Look up 1 John 2:3-6. Read these verses.*
- What questions come to mind? How did you search for the meaning of the text?
- Maybe you asked some questions like this:
  1. What are Jesus' commands? (Look up the word *command* in the New Testament to see what Jesus said. *Hint: John 14:15, John 15:12*)
  2. Who are those who "have come to know Him"?
  3. How do we keep His Word?
  4. How did Jesus walk? How should I walk?

## BIBLE MEMORY

One way to renew our minds with Scripture is to commit Bible verses to memory. This week's memory verse is Matthew 4:4. Practice different ways to memorize this verse. You could recite it with a friend, make up a game or hand motions, or write it out a few times. Whatever method you use, memorizing Scripture will always be rewarding and help keep your mind fixed on Jesus.

_____

_____

_____

_____

**Transformation**
Changed outwardly or inwardly; In the Bible, transformation often results from an encounter with God in Christ.

# DAILY DISCIPLESHIP

Here are a few tips as you read God's Word and use the journal pages to write down what you learn:

- What does the text say? Write down exact truths from the Bible.

- Let Scripture interpret Scripture. What do these verses mean? Be careful to not insert your own meaning into the text.

- How can you apply the truths of God's Word to your life? How should these truths change the way you think and live?

## DAY ONE

*The Bible leads us to God.*

- *Read Ephesians 4:17-20; Ephesians 2:1-3; Ephesians 2:12-13; and 1 Peter 1:18-19.*

We should care what the Bible says because it leads us to know God more. Before we knew Jesus and believed in Him as Savior, we were separated from God because of our sin. Our minds were focused on things of the world that were futile or useless. We did not have a right understanding and our hearts were hardened to the truth. We chased after the things we wanted, rather than Jesus. The way we lived did not reflect the holiness of God. However, those who are saved by grace learned about Jesus at some point! Someone shared the good news of God's Word with us, and our eyes were opened to the truth.

- How do these verses contrast the life of the believer before believing in Jesus and after believing in Jesus?

- How could neglecting God's Word lead us to temptation to sin?

## DAY TWO

*The Bible is good news.*

● *Read Ephesians 4:20-21; Ephesians 1:13; Colossians 1:5-6; and James 1:21.*

What's some of the best news you've ever received? Maybe it was hearing you would be going to an exciting new place, or that your parents finally bought you a gift you've been wanting. We all like to receive good news because it brings us joy! The Bible brings us the best news of all. When we read or hear God's Word, we find the true way to salvation. There's no better news than that! We first believed in Jesus because we heard the good news of the gospel. We should care what the Bible says because only the Bible leads us to Jesus.

● How can you share this good news with others?

_____

_____

_____

● Why is it important to read the Bible and be reminded of the good news of the gospel?

_____

_____

## DAY THREE

*The Bible renews our minds.*

● *Read Ephesians 4:21-23; Colossians 2:6-7; Psalm 51:10; Philippians 4:8; and 2 Corinthians 10:5.*

Did you know that our brains have roughly 70,000 thoughts per day? That's a lot of thinking going on! While many thoughts are barely remembered, we do create thought patterns in our brain. Choosing to train our brains to think on what is good and right and holy is important for believers. What's more, the thoughts our minds dwell on often reveal what we desire most. If we let our hearts and minds go unchecked, it won't be long before we are tempted to sin through our words and

continued on next page >

actions. God has promised that He is making us into new creations, but we must obey God's Word to renew our minds so that we are walking with the Spirit.

●  What do these verses say about how we renew our minds?

_____

_____

●  What thoughts should occupy our hearts and minds?

_____

## DAY FOUR

*The Bible sanctifies us.*

●  *Read Ephesians 4:22-24; Galatians 2:20; 1 Peter 1:13-16 and 22-23; and John 15:1-4.*

Our sin is forgiven when we place our faith in Jesus, but the temptation to sin is not fully gone. We continue to sin because we have a sinful nature, but when Jesus returns, He will make us sinless like Him. We still struggle with temptations, and the sin we hate still plagues us. However, looking to Jesus through God's Word helps us to fight the sin that so easily trips us up. God promised that He will continue to sanctify us, or make us look more and more like Jesus. Still, we have a role to play in our sanctification. We must be obedient to God's Word and abide in Jesus.

●  How does Jesus live through us and help us to look more like Him?

_____

_____

_____

●  What does it mean to be holy?

_____

_____

_____

## DAY FIVE

*The Bible reminds us to be like God.*

● *Read Ephesians 4:24-32; 2 Peter 1:2-4; 1 John 1:9; and 2 Timothy 2:21.*

Our culture often uses the phrases "do you" or "be you." While the sentiment of being yourself or being who God made you is a good thing, we have to be careful to not approve sinful behavior as an excuse for "being ourselves." God has called us to be holy and set apart for His glory. The Bible reminds us of who God is and who we are to imitate. We walk in a manner pleasing to God when we act or speak as He would. We point others to Jesus when our lives mirror God.

● What does a holy life look like?

_____

_____

_____

● What should we do when we mess up or act unholy?

_____

_____

## JOURNAL & PRAYER

_____

_____

_____

_____

_____

_____

_____

Do not be conformed to this age, but be transformed by the renewing of your mind, so that you may discern what is the good, pleasing, and perfect will of God.

### Romans 12:2

# DOES THE BIBLE REALLY TELL ME ALL I NEED TO KNOW?

The Bible tells us that Jesus supplies our every need.

## 🔒 KEY PASSAGE

*Matthew 19:16-26*

## 🔑 KEY VERSE

*2 Peter 1:3*

## WHICH CAME FIRST?

In each pair listed, circle what you think came first.

| | |
|---|---|
| the chicken | the egg |
| trees | oxygen |
| watermelon seeds | watermelons |

In today's Bible study, we will see that ultimately Jesus meets all of our needs, both for salvation and for living a godly life.

# SHARPEN & STRENGTHEN

Our hearts can easily deceive us into believing that we need something other than Jesus in order to earn salvation or be happy. However, the Bible points us to a Savior who is more than enough. Only in Jesus do we find everything we need. Jesus does the impossible by reconciling sinners to a holy God and also helping us to live a godly life for His glory. Will you turn to Jesus this week and allow Him to supply your every need?

### Are we good enough?

- *Read Matthew 19:16-19.*
- Have you ever tried to be good for God? Have you ever thought you could make God love you more by the good things you do? *Hint: You can write in code if you don't want anyone to read your answer.*

---

### How does the law reveal our shortcomings?

- *Read Matthew 19:20-22.*
- Decode the message by cracking the code! *Hint: replace each letter with the letter that comes after it in the alphabet. In this code "A" comes after "Z"!*

It is _ _ _ _ _ who _ _ _ _ _ _ _ _ _ our _ _ _ _ _ _
     I  D  R  T  R      R  Z  S  H  R  E  H  D  R      G  D  Z  Q  S  R

and _ _ _ _ _ _ _ us from _ _ _ and _ _ _ _ _ .
    Q  D  R  B  T  D  R      R  H  M      C  D  Z  S  G

### Who then can be saved?

- *Read Matthew 19:23-26.*
- Fill in the blank:

    1. Jesus gives us _____ when we don't know what to do.
       (See Col. 2:3.)

    2. Jesus gives us _____ to endure hardships and glorify God in trials. (See Phil. 4:13.)

    3. Jesus _____ _____ _____ so that we may live rightly. (See John 1:14.)

    4. Jesus shows us how we should _____ and _____ for

       _____ . (See 1 John 4:19.)

continued on next page >

5. Jesus will _____ our every need, both for _____

and _____ a life that _____ _____ _____

_____ . (See Phil. 4:19.)

# FIRE IT UP!

## GODLY LIVING

- *Read 2 Peter 1:3.*
- What does godly living look like at your school, sports team, in your home, and so forth?

_____

_____

_____

- How can we live a godly life? (See also 2 Timothy 1:9.)

_____

_____

- How does living a godly life glorify God?

**The fall**
The coming of sin
into the world

_____

_____

_____

## OUR GREATEST TREASURE

Our culture chases after many different treasures. Like the rich young ruler, some may love their wealth more than anything. For others, they may treasure success. What are some treasures that you have seen people chase after? Fill the blanks below with a list of things our culture treasures:

_____        _____

_____        _____

Look up the following verses and write down how Jesus is our greatest treasure, and only in Him will we be fully satisfied.

- Philippians 3:8-10 _____

- John 10:10 _____

- Mark 8:36 _____

- Psalm 103:1-5 _____

- Psalm 16:11 _____

- Hebrews 13:5 _____

- Psalm 63:1-5 _____

- John 6:35 _____

- John 7:38 _____

- Psalm 107:9 _____

The Bible tells me that Jesus supplies my every need.

## JESUS SUPPLIES ALL OUR NEEDS

Jesus died on the cross and was resurrected so that we may have eternal life, and also so that we may live life for God's glory here on earth. Jesus has given us the Holy Spirit and His Word to help us as we live out our faith.

- What happens when we are faced with a situation that is not answered in Scripture? How does Jesus and the Bible help us to navigate tough questions?

Jesus never promised that He will give us every answer. However, He did promise to give us wisdom and to be with us always. When you are faced with tough situations, remember that Jesus will supply your every need.

# DAILY DISCIPLESHIP

Here are a few tips as you read God's Word and use the journal pages to write down what you learn:

- What does the text say? Write down exact truths from the Bible.
- Let Scripture interpret Scripture. What do these verses mean? Be careful to not insert your own meaning into the text.
- How can you apply the truths of God's Word to your life? How should these truths change the way you think and live?

## DAY ONE

*Only God is good.*

- *Read Matthew 19:16-17; Psalm 25:7-11; Matthew 5:48; and Psalm 92:15.*

We all like to think that we are pretty good. We mostly do this by comparing ourselves with others who we think are "bad." Even when we read the Bible, we see the sin of Israel or Judas or Peter and think they were worse than we are. However, Jesus makes it very clear that no one but God is good. Jesus often used the word *good* to mean holy, perfect, fully righteous, and without any sin. Only God fits this standard. We can never measure up to the perfection of God. God's holiness is important to understand because it gives us a right view of ourselves. When we stand next to a holy God, we can't help but say as Isaiah did, "Woe is me!" (See Isaiah 6:5.) No matter how much good we try to do, we can never attain the holiness of God on our own.

- How does the holiness of God show sinners like us the way?

_____

_____

_____

**Rationalize**
Attempting to explain or justify your behavior with logical reasons, even if they are not true

- How can God ask us to be holy if we are sinners?

_____

_____

_____

## DAY TWO

*The Bible shows us God's holy standard.*

● *Read Matthew 19:18-19; 1 Peter 1:16; Psalm 12:6; Matthew 22:37; and Proverbs 16:11.*

Have you ever been given an expectation that you didn't measure up to? Sometimes our teachers, parents, or even friends set expectations for us that we end up failing. In a similar way, God gave Israel the Ten Commandments so they would live according to God's holy standards. Israel (and us!) could not keep all of the commands. The law shows us our need for Jesus. In our culture, it might seem foreign or weird to have a standard or guideline by which someone should live. Most people want to live their own way, doing what seems right or feels right to them. Yet God has told us that we are to be holy because He is holy. The Bible helps us see the holiness of God and the means by which we should live.

● What are some ways it can be hard to live according to God's standards?

_____

_____

_____

● What are some ways God's Word tells us we should live?

_____

_____

_____

## DAY THREE

*The law reveals our sin.*

● *Read Matthew 19:20-22; Romans 7:7-13; James 2:10; and Romans 3:20.*

If you've ever looked at 3D optical illusion (stereogram), you know that when you first view the image, it looks like a bunch of colors. You can't see the hidden image within the chaos of colors and patterns. However, by refocusing our eyes in a different way, the image suddenly pops out! In a similar way, when we first look at our hearts, we don't always see the sin hidden there. Yet, when we look to God's Word, we are able to see

continued on next page >

that we do not measure up to God's holiness. The law was never meant to save us—it was meant to reveal our sin and show how we fall short of God's holiness.

● Can we be justified (saved) through the law? Why or why not?

● How does the law show us our sin?

## DAY FOUR

*We cannot save ourselves.*

● *Read Matthew 19:23-25; Romans 4:1-5; Ephesians 2:8-10; Romans 3:28; and Galatians 2:16.*

It is impossible for us to save ourselves from our sins. No matter how many good deeds we do or how we may think we are not as "bad" as others, there is no way we can earn our salvation. Many other religions and cultural worldviews have some form of a works-based faith. That is to say, if you live a certain way or don't do certain things, then you will find eternal life or spiritual awakening. However, our good deeds are filthy rags compared to a holy God. (See Isaiah 64:6.) Sometimes our actions reveal the fruit of our faith, but the actions themselves cannot save us.

● How can you explain to others that a person can never be good enough to earn salvation?

● How are we justified if not by works? (See Rom. 3:24.)

## DAY FIVE

*God does the impossible.*

- *Read Matthew 19:25-26; Job 42:2; Jeremiah 32:17; Acts 4:12; 2 Timothy 1:9; and Titus 2:11-12.*

It is impossible for us to save ourselves, but with God, all things are possible. Nothing is too hard for our great God! We could never be so bad that God's grace in Jesus would not forgive our sins. God's free gift of salvation through Jesus is offered to all who would believe in His name. All we must do is repent and believe! God's grace also helps us to live a holy life now. The more we look to Jesus and what He did for us on the cross, the more we desire to live for Him. His love for us changes our desires from self-serving to God-honoring.

- What must we say "no" to in order to live a godly life?

_____

_____

- How can we share God's gift of salvation with others?

_____

_____

_____

## JOURNAL & PRAYER

_____

_____

_____

_____

Check out these verses too!

Philippians 4:6 & 19
Matthew 6:33; 7:11
James 1:5
1 Corinthians 1:30

# IS HEAVEN REAL?

The Bible tells us what is true about eternal life.

## KEY PASSAGES

*John 6:38-42;*
*2 Corinthians 5:1-10;*
*Revelation 21:9-27*

## KEY VERSE

*Philippians 3:20-21*

## JUST FOR FUN

If you could live anywhere in the world, where would it be? Why there?

What would your house be like?

Who would you want your neighbors to be?

# SHARPEN & STRENGTHEN

One day, those who trust in Jesus as Savior will be united with Him forever. Because of this, we are a people of great hope, because death is not the final victor. Not only do we have a Savior who conquered death, but Jesus also went to prepare a place for us with Him in heaven. It is our joy to long to be with God and dwell with Him. One day, Jesus will return and make all things new. As we walk this earth by faith, we set our minds on things to come and wait eagerly for the new heavens and new earth where God's creation will be renewed. Our eternal home will be the most beautiful city, filled with all joy and satisfaction in Jesus. Let us live in light of eternity and choose to tell others about the good news of Jesus Christ.

*Is heaven an actual place?*

● *Read John 6:38-42.*

_____ is a real place where God most fully reveals His glory, and where angels, other heavenly creatures, and redeemed Christians all worship Him.

The _____ _____ and _____ _____ describes the entirely renewed creation where believers will dwell with God forever. One day Jesus will return and make all things new.

*What happens when we die?*

● *Read 2 Corinthians 5:1-10.*

● How does looking forward to heaven help us live for Jesus now?

_____

_____

*What is eternity like?*

● *Read Revelation 21:9-27.*

● What are some ways you have heard people describe heaven?

_____

_____

● Our eternal home will be the most joy-filled, all-satisfying, perfectly good city. There will be no sadness or sin or pain. Everything that once was will be made new and perfect.

# FIRE IT UP!

## IMAGINE IT!

*Read Revelation 21:9-27 and Revelation 22:1-5. Using these verses, draw a picture of the new heavens and new earth as a city.*

## THERE'S A PLACE FOR YOU IN HEAVEN

In John 14:1-6, Jesus speaks of heaven as a very real place. Jesus came from heaven, and Jesus returned to heaven. (See Acts 1:11.) Jesus also wants us to join Him there one day.

- *Read John 14:1-6 and answer the following questions.*
- When Jesus left the earth, what was He going to do?


- How does this promise give us hope? (See 1 Peter 1:3-5.)

- Will we be with Jesus in heaven? How do we know that is true? (See John 14:3 and Ephesians 2:6.)

_____

_____

_____

- What is the only way to heaven?

_____

_____

_____

> The Bible tells me what is true about eternal life.

## WHO NEEDS TO KNOW JESUS?

Every person has a decision to make. Will they follow Jesus or reject Him? God desires that all people come to saving faith, and He has given us the mission to share the good news of the gospel. Make a list of people you can pray for and tell about Jesus.

_____  _____

_____  _____

_____  _____

_____  _____

_____  _____

_____

_____

_____

### Heaven
A real place where God most fully reveals His glory, and where angels, other heavenly creatures, and redeemed Christians all worship Him

# DAILY DISCIPLESHIP

Here are a few tips as you read God's Word and use the journal pages to write down what you learn:

- What does the text say? Write down exact truths from the Bible.
- Let Scripture interpret Scripture. What do these verses mean? Be careful to not insert your own meaning into the text.
- How can you apply the truths of God's Word to your life? How should these truths change the way you think and live?

## DAY ONE

*Heaven is God's dwelling place.*

- *Read John 6:38-42; John 3:13; Deuteronomy 26:15; Philippians 1:23; and Revelation 21:3-4.*

When people talk about heaven, they usually refer to a place up in the sky that we cannot see and where we will once again see friends and family members who trusted in Jesus and have died. In part, this is true. We cannot see heaven, and heaven is often referred to a place above us. All those who have trusted in Jesus will be gathered together to worship Him. The Bible does not tell us exactly where heaven is, but it does say that heaven is where God dwells and most fully reveals His glory. In fact, without God, heaven would not be anything special at all. What makes heaven so beautiful and a place we desire to be is God's eternal presence! Being joined to Jesus will bring us more joy than any of the other wonderful aspects of heaven.

- Where did Jesus say He came from?

_____

- Does Paul desire to depart and be in heaven or be with Jesus? Why?

_____

_____

_____

_____

**New heavens & new earth**
The entirely renewed creation where believers will dwell with God forever; one day Jesus will return and make all things new

## DAY TWO

*Heaven is a place for Christians.*

● *Read John 6:38-42; 1 John 5:13; Matthew 7:13-14; 2 Corinthians 5:21; and 1 John 1:9.*

Many people believe that when they die, they go to heaven, as if heaven is just the natural destination for all people...unless, of course, you're really bad. However, this is not what the Bible teaches. In fact, because of our sin, our default destination is hell. Since heaven is God's dwelling place—perfect, holy, and without sin—only people who are righteous may enter in. On our own, we have no righteousness, but through faith in Jesus, our sins are forgiven and His righteousness is placed on us. Thus, only those who have repented of their sin and trusted in Jesus as their Savior can go to heaven.

● Why doesn't everyone go to heaven? What about people who are really nice and help a lot of people?

● How does Jesus make us righteous?

## DAY THREE

*Heaven is our true home.*

● *Read 2 Corinthians 5:1-10; Hebrews 11:16; and 2 Peter 3:13.*

If you've ever been away from home for a long time, you know what it is like to be homesick. When you finally return, it's the best feeling! All of your comforts and familiarities are restored. You feel like you are where you belong. However, for some, home can be an unfamiliar word. Those who have moved around a lot or never really felt connected to one place may have a hard time understanding the feeling of being home. Yet everyone who is saved will know they are home when enter into God's presence. In the presence of Jesus, we will find rest and comfort, knowing

continued on next page >

we are finally where we belong. Even now, we look forward to our final home in the new heavens and new earth, longing to be joined to our Savior King. Our time on this earth is important, and God has a purpose for us, but what a glorious day it will be when Jesus returns and makes all things new.

● What does Paul mean when he says "we groan"? (2 Corinthians 5:2)

● Why will the new heavens and new earth be a better home?

## DAY FOUR

*Heaven will become the new heavens and earth.*

● *Read Revelation 21:9-27; Isaiah 65:17; Revelation 21:3; Ephesians 1:10; and Isaiah 51:3.*

One day Jesus will return and defeat sin and death once and for all. After this, He will create a new heaven and earth. God will eternally join His space (heaven) to Earth. In this new realm, everything will be made new. There will be no sin or pain or sadness. God will make the new heaven and earth the most beautiful and good place to ever exist. We will see familiar faces and feast on the best food. Nature will be more vibrant and filled with many wonders. The city of God will be a city like no other, full of jewels and precious metals. We will have no need of the sun because Jesus' glory will be our light. The best part is that God will dwell with us forever!

● What ideas have you heard about heaven that didn't quite line up with the Bible?

- How does this new picture of heaven and earth bring you hope and increase your longing for it?

_____

_____

## DAY FIVE

*Heaven is a city of nations worshiping God.*

- *Read Revelation 21:9-27; Isaiah 60:3-4; Revelation 5:11-14; Revelation 7:9-12; and Revelation 19:6-7.*

Sadly, when people think of heaven, they often believe that it will be like a boring church service—singing hymns all the time and floating around on clouds, but this is not at all how the Bible describes worship in heaven. Worship is not just the singing of songs or hearing the Bible preached—worship stems from everything we do. We worship God in spirit and in truth when we go for a bike ride and praise Him for the joy of His creation. We worship God when we thank Him for food that tastes delicious and leaves us satisfied. We worship God when we enjoy new experiences and thank Him for His goodness. In heaven, worship will be the natural overflow of our hearts because we will enjoy ultimate fellowship with Him. We will also hear and experience the worship of God from every tribe, nation, and language. It will be the most amazing time of our lives and we will never tire of it.

- How do you worship God now?

_____

_____

- How do these verses help you think about worship in heaven?

_____

_____

_____

_____

Hallelujah, because our Lord God, the Almighty, reigns!

**Revelation 19:6**

# WILL GOD REALLY JUDGE ME?

The Bible tells us what is true about judgment.

## 🔒 KEY PASSAGES

*Luke 16:19-31;*
*Revelation 20:11-15*

## 🔑 KEY VERSE

*Numbers 14:18*

## FEAR RATING SCALE

Rate these fears from 1-10, use your imagination for the one at the bottom!

*Ah! Where my blankie*

You hear a weird noise at night.

1  2  3  4  5  6  7  8  9  10

A big dog barks at you from across the street.

*Not scary at all.*

1  2  3  4  5  6  7  8  9  10

A hundred baby spiders are born and crawl on your bed.

1  2  3  4  5  6  7  8  9  10

Your friend just dropped your new phone in the swimming pool.

1  2  3  4  5  6  7  8  9  10

1  2  3  4  5  6  7  8  9  10

# SHARPEN & STRENGTHEN

Have you ever feared being judged? At some point in our lives, we have probably experienced judgment from others. And chances are, that judgment did not make us feel very good. However, God stands as the supreme Judge. Only His verdict will matter when we stand to give an account of our lives. Yet those who belong to Jesus have no need to fear.

### Why do faith and works matter?

- *Read Luke 16:19-23.*
- Complete the phrase below by unscrambling the words under each blank.

Only those who are _____ by _____ in
                     v s a d e                   h t f i a

_____ will enter _____ .
       u s J s e                     n h v e e a

### Is God's judgment really just?

- *Read Luke 16:24-31.*
- What is meant by God is "holy"?

_____

_____

**God's holiness**
The intrinsic worth, beauty, purity, value, and excellence of God; God is above all else; nothing is like Him

### What will the final judgment be like?

- *Read Revelation 20:11-15.*
- According to these verses, what are the books that were opened?

_____

_____

_____

_____

_____

> What good is it, my brothers and sisters, if someone claims to have faith but does not have works? Can such faith save him. If a brother or sister is without clothes and lacks daily food and one of you says to them, "Go in peace, stay warm, and be well fed," but you don't give them what the body needs, what good is it? In the same way faith, if it doesn't have works, is dead by itself.
>
> **James 2:14-17**

# FIRE IT UP!

## GOD'S PERFECT JUDGMENT & GRACE

Look up the following Bible verses and write down God's judgment and also how God showed grace.

| Bible Verse | Judgment | Grace |
|---|---|---|
| Genesis 3:14-15 | | |
| Genesis 6:5-7, 17-18 | | |
| Exodus 6:6-8; 12:12-13 | | |
| Numbers 21:4-6, 8-9 | | |
| Isaiah 3:8-9; 14:1-2 | | |

## FRUITS OF FAITH

**Works**
Right actions that give evidence of genuine faith and transformation that has occurred in the life of a believer

God says that we should love our neighbor as ourselves. Despite who our neighbors are, what they look like, or how they act, we are commanded to love them just as Jesus loved us. By showing love for our neighbor, we are proving our love for God to be true. Read each of the scenarios with your group, then discuss how you might show your love for these individuals.

1. A friend is struggling with some family issues. Her parents have been fighting a lot, and she's

having a hard time focusing on school. She's often sad and feels alone.

2. A man in your neighborhood just found out he lost his job. He's older and doesn't have any other family around to help take care of him. You often see him taking his dog for a walk but have never really taken the time to speak with him.

3. The school bully just found out that his mom has cancer. He's always been mean and picked on others, and this news has made everything worse. He's hurting but doesn't know how to deal with his pain.

## DOUBTING OUR SALVATION

Thinking about the judgment of God can make us wonder if our name will be written in the book of life. Every follower of Christ will experience times of doubt in her faith. Sometimes those doubts lead us to question our salvation. We may think we don't obey like we should, or we compare ourselves to other believers and think that they are doing a lot better than us. Our faith may seem stagnant and lead us to question if God really even saved us in the first place.

However, the Bible teaches that in Jesus our salvation is secure, and not only that, but it is Jesus who will help us to persist and stand firm in our faith. If we begin to doubt our salvation, there are a few good questions we can ask and many Bible verses to help us.

1. Does my heart desire God and the things of God?

2. Is there evidence of faith in my life? Is the Holy Spirit leading me?

3. Am I fully trusting in Jesus and looking to Him to help me when I fail?

Read the following verses and write the truths of assurance given to us in God's Word:

● Romans 8:1-2

● Philippians 1:6

● 1 Thessalonians 5:23-24

● 1 Corinthians 1:8-9

● Romans 8:13-16

# DAILY DISCIPLESHIP

Here are a few tips as you read God's Word and use the journal pages to write down what you learn:

- What does the text say? Write down exact truths from the Bible.
- Let Scripture interpret Scripture. What do these verses mean? Be careful to not insert your own meaning into the text.
- How can you apply the truths of God's Word to your life? How should these truths change the way you think and live?

## DAY ONE

*This world and its desires will pass away.*

- *Read Luke 16:19-25; 1 John 2:15,17; Romans 13:14; 1 Peter 4:7-11; and Matthew 6:19-21.*

At times we all desire things of this world. Maybe we crave the praise of other people, or maybe we love money and possessions. Even food can become a desire that steals the place of God. Any desires we have that replace God as our greatest treasure are idols. While these things may bring pleasure or make us happy for awhile, they will eventually be destroyed. Only when we repent and look to Jesus will we find pleasures that never end. (See Psalm 16:11.) In Luke 16, the rich man sought what he wanted above all else. If we're not intentional about thinking about what happens after we die, we too can get swept up in only thinking about the things of this world. Randy Alcorn wrote, "Our minds are so much set on Earth that we are unaccustomed to heavenly thinking. So we must work at it."[2]

- Why must we look past this world and look forward to what is eternal?

- What is eternal? What things will last?

## DAY TWO

*Judgment has only two destinations.*

- *Read Luke 16:22-26; Isaiah 66:24; Matthew 25:41-46; Romans 2:7-8; and John 6:47.*

If you've ever boarded an airplane, you've handed the flight attendant your ticket with your final destination written on it. You were headed to one final place. In a similar way, when we stand before God, our "ticket" will have one final destination. There are no refunds, do-overs, or stops along the way. Our names will either be written in the book of life or they will not. Yet while we are here on this earth, we are given the opportunity to respond to Jesus' offer of salvation. Hell will be a place of torment because God and His goodness will not dwell there. On the other hand, heaven will be a place of pure joy, and the greatest of adventures await us there. However, we don't look forward to heaven to avoid hell. We look forward to heaven because Jesus is there, and He is what will make heaven so great!

- How do these verses describe hell?

- What determines where we end up?

## DAY THREE

*We are called to share the gospel.*

- *Read Luke 16:27-31; Acts 26:22-23; Romans 1:16; Romans 10:14-15; and Mark 16:15.*

Thinking about God's just judgment should motivate us to share the gospel with others. We want to warn others about hell because we want them to know Jesus who loves them unconditionally. While we don't often like to talk about Hell, it would be unloving to not warn others about the suffering that awaits people who reject Jesus. Just as we would warn others about a potential danger, like not boarding a plane you knew was going to crash, we should speak truth about God's judgment in love.

continued on next page >

Jesus has given us the command to preach the gospel to all the world. Whether we travel around the world or go to school with unbelievers, we are to share with others about a God who saves and loves the people He created. After all, we were all created to love God and enjoy Him forever. Only in heaven will we be able to do just that.

- Who helps us as we share the good news of the gospel?

- Why should we not fear sharing Jesus with others?

## DAY FOUR

*Jesus is the only righteous Judge.*

- *Read Revelation 20:11-15; Acts 10:42; Romans 2:6-11; John 12:47-48; and 2 Timothy 4:8.*

Jesus' primary mission in coming into the world was to seek and save the lost. He came as the Suffering Servant, a sacrifice for our sins. The Bible teaches us that Jesus is also Judge. In fact, He is the only righteous Judge worthy of declaring who shall be rewarded for their faith and who shall be condemned for rejecting Him. Jesus knows all the intentions of our heart and the works we have done. He shows no partiality, but judges in absolute fairness. Those who have trusted in Him as Savior have nothing to fear from His judgment. His sacrifice on the cross paid the penalty for our sin. In fact, we are to look forward to His coming as Judge and King, when He will appear in all His glory. One day, every knee will bow and every tongue will confess that Jesus is Lord.

- What reward(s) will we receive from Judge Jesus?

- How will Jesus judge all people?

## DAY FIVE

*Jesus has secured our salvation.*

- *Read Revelation 20:11-15; Revelation 3:5; John 5:24; John 10:28; and Romans 8:38-39.*

If we are followers of Jesus, we have no need to fear the day of judgment, nor do we need to worry that our names will not be written in the book of life. God's Word gives us the assurance that if we are followers of Jesus, He will never let us fall away from our faith. We will persevere to the end because He will help us to do so. God's love for us is so great that nothing could ever separate us from His love for us. We can be hopeful, trusting that we have a good God who is faithful and secures our salvation.

- How does God's love for us give us eternal hope?

- What will Jesus say about us before God the Father?

## JOURNAL & PRAYER

The Bible tells me what is true about judgment.

# HOW CAN I BE USED BY GOD?

The Bible tells us what is true about God's mission for us.

## KEY PASSAGE

Acts 17:16-34

## KEY VERSE

Romans 10:14-15

## HALF & HALF

Complete the drawings of different tools below.

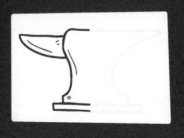

# SHARPEN & STRENGTHEN

Did you know that believers have been given a job from God? God has provided everything we need to live on mission for Him through His Word. God will use everyone who wants to follow Him and obediently do His will.

### *Do I have a heart for the lost?*

- *Read Acts 17:16-21.*
- What are some ways the Holy Spirit has moved your heart to care for the lost?

> Then he said to his disciples, "The harvest is abundant, but the workers are few. Therefore, pray to the Lord of the harvest to send out workers into his harvest."
>
> ### Matthew 9:37-38

### *How do I know what to say?*

- *Read Acts 17:22-31.*
- What is the gospel?

The gospel is the truth about who Jesus is (the Son of God/fully God and fully man) and what He did (lived a perfect life, died on the cross for our sins, and rose again)

### *What if people mock me?*

- *Read Acts 17:32-34.*
- Have you or someone you know ever been mocked for believing in Jesus? How did you persevere?

**God's mission**
the plan and purpose of God among us to glorify Himself through the work of redeeming people and restoring His creation

# FIRE IT UP!

## TELL YOUR STORY

Has Jesus changed your life? If so, you have a testimony of faith. Through Jesus, we are brought from death to life. Think about your life before Jesus, how the gospel came to you, and how Jesus has changed your life through the gospel. Write your story below.

If you have not yet placed faith in Jesus, then look up the following verses and write out the gospel. (See The Gospel: God's Plan for Me on page 111 for reference.) Ask God to help you believe and trust in Jesus. (John 3:16; Romans 3:23; 1 Peter 3:18; Romans 5:8; 1 Corinthians 15:3-6; Titus 3:4-7; Ephesians 2:1-10)

The Bible tells me what is true abou God's mission for me.

**Lost**
Term used in the Bible to refer to people who have not trusted in Jesus as Lord and Savior

## FEAR NOT!

We do not need to fear sharing our faith with others, but sometimes fear creeps into our hearts and keeps us from being obedient. Look up the following verses and write a brief summary of why God has called us not to fear.

- John 14:2 _____

- Joshua 1:9 _____

- Psalm 94:19 _____

- Romans 8:38-39 _____

- Psalm 27:1 _____

- Isaiah 41:10 _____

- 2 Timothy 1:7 _____

- 1 John 4:18 _____

## GOD SO LOVED THE WORLD

The International Mission Board (IMB) is an organization partnering with churches to help a lost world know Jesus. They have provided many resources to learn more about God's heart for the nations and how we can join God on His mission. Watch the video with your group created by the IMB to learn more about God's love for the world. Then write ways you can be on mission with Him.

_____

_____

_____

_____

### Gospel
The truth about who Jesus is (the Son of God/fully God and fully man) and what He did (lived a perfect life, died on the cross for our sins, and rose again)

# DAILY DISCIPLESHIP

Here are a few tips as you read God's Word and use the journal pages to write down what you learn:

- What does the text say? Write down exact truths from the Bible.
- Let Scripture interpret Scripture. What do these verses mean? Be careful to not insert your own meaning into the text.
- How can you apply the truths of God's Word to your life? How should these truths change the way you think and live?

## DAY ONE

*God can use you to love the lost.*

- *Read Acts 17:16-17; 2 Peter 3:9; Luke 4:18-19; and Mark 2:17.*

Have you ever judged someone who doesn't know Jesus? Sometimes we see the sin of other lost people and think poorly of them. Rather than be saddened about their blindness to their sin, we feel contempt. Paul's reaction to the men of Athens was not one of hatred, but of compassion. He saw their idols and knew they needed to be set free from the slavery of sin. He preached the gospel—not out of a sense of self-righteousness, but out of love for them. Paul had a heart for the lost because He knew God loves the lost. In fact, at some point, we were all far off from God. It is only because someone loved us and told us the truth about Jesus that we believed and trusted in Him.

- How do these verses show God's heart for the lost?

_____

_____

- What can we do to show love for all people?

_____

_____

_____

_____

## DAY TWO

*God can use you to reason with others.*

● *Read Acts 17:17-21; 2 Corinthians 5:11; 2 Corinthians 4:5-6; and Luke 14:23.*

The gospel of Jesus is both true and reasonable. It is not crazy to believe that there is a God who created the world and redeemed us from our sin. Part of sharing the good news is to have conversations with others and help them see that it is foolish to not believe in Jesus. God can use each of us to propose rational arguments that persuade others to believe in Jesus. Paul reasoned with the men of Athens by showing them that they were right to worship, but that they were worshiping the wrong gods. As Paul shared, some were persuaded to hear more. By sharing our faith calmly, lovingly, truthfully, and passionately, we can have conversations with others that lead to a desire to know more about Jesus.

● How is it reasonable to believe in Jesus?

● Why does Jesus say that we should compel people to come to faith? (See Luke 14:23.)

## DAY THREE

*God can use you to show others only God deserves our worship.*

● *Read Acts 17:22-29; John 4:22-23; Acts 14:15; Exodus 20:3; and Philippians 2:9-11.*

We were all made to worship. The problem lies in what we choose to worship. The men of Athens crafted idols of stone and metals to worship, but Paul told them that they were made to worship the one true God. He said, "In Him we live and move and have our being" (Acts 17:28). In

continued on next page >

other words, God created you; therefore you should worship Him only. Likewise, we can tell others that it is only God who deserves to be loved above all else. By pointing others to a God who created us and sustains us, we can show others that He alone is to be worshiped.

● How are we to worship God?

● Why is God alone worthy of our worship?

## DAY FOUR

*God can use you to call people to repentance and faith.*

● *Read Acts 17:30-31; Mark 1:15; 1 John 1:9; 2 Timothy 2:25; 2 Corinthians 7:10; and Romans 2:4.*

Sometimes people do not think they are sinners. Other times people think they are so bad, God could never love them. Both of these views are wrong. Everyone is a sinner, but no one is too far off that God could not save them. Paul knew that these men were sinners just like him, and he called them to repentance. He called them to turn away from false gods to the God of truth. Likewise, we are to call people to repentance. Without turning away from our sin and seeking Jesus for forgiveness, there is no genuine faith. We can lovingly call people to repent and help them know there is a God who wants to forgive them.

● Why must we repent?

● How does God's kindness lead us to repentance?

## DAY FIVE

*God can use you to lead people to salvation.*

- *Read Acts 17:32-34; Revelation 3:20; Titus 3:5; Romans 10:9-10; and John 1:12.*

The joy we experience in leading someone to Christ is like no other. When someone trusts in Jesus as their Lord and Savior, they are brought from death to life. What could be better than that? God has called followers of Jesus to preach His good news so that people will hear and believe in Jesus. Paul preached and people believed. It was not Paul who saved anyone—God does that—but Paul was obedient to follow Jesus' command to make His truth known. We too can lead people to salvation, but only if we choose to obey Jesus' commands.

- How do these verses help us understand how Jesus saves?

- Who can you share the gospel with?

## JOURNAL & PRAYER

# HOW DO I KEEP FOLLOWING JESUS WHEN THINGS ARE DIFFICULT?

The Bible tells us what is true about following Jesus.

## 🔒 KEY PASSAGES

*Luke 14:25-33;*
*Matthew 13:44-45;*
*James 1:2-4, 12*

## 🔑 KEY VERSE

*Philippians 3:8*

## ROLLIN' IN IT

What is one item you really want to buy right now?

How much money would it cost you to get it?

In today's Bible study, Jesus described the cost of following Him. If Jesus truly is our greatest treasure, then we should desire to follow Him no matter what it might cost us.

# SHARPEN & STRENGTHEN

*Do I love Jesus more than anything?*

● *Read Luke 14:25-27.*

● Why do you think Jesus used the example of family and ourselves in comparing love for Him above all else?

_____

_____

*What will it cost me to follow Jesus?*

● *Read Luke 14:28-33.*

● How do we let go of the attachments of this world to follow Jesus no matter what it may cost?

_____

*Is Jesus worth the cost?*

● *Read Matthew 13:44-45.*

● Why should we joyfully endure trials?

_____

● *Read James 1:2-4;12.*

● Decode the message of hope below. *Hint: use the first letter of each picture to fill in the missing letters.*

When we _ _ _ _ _ _   _ _ _ _ _ _ _ _ —and we will—

we should do so _ _ _ _   _ _ _ ' _ _ _ _ _ _ _ _,

that _ _ _ _ _ _ is _ _ _ _ _ _ _ _.

# FIRE IT UP!

## THE LOSS OF ALL THINGS

Philippians 3:8 is this week's key verse. Rewrite the verse substituting "everything" and "all things" with things that might be hard for you to lose. Remember that Jesus is worthy of any sacrifice, and in Him, we will gain far more than we will ever lose.

> *More than that, I also consider **everything** to be a loss in view of the surpassing value of knowing Christ Jesus my Lord. Because of him I have suffered the loss of **all things** and consider them as dung, so that I may gain Christ. Philippians 3:8*

The Bible tel me what is true about following Jesus.

Remember that Jesus is worthy of any sacrifice and that in Him we will gain far more than we will ever lose.

## A PROMISE FAR BETTER

*Read Hebrews 11:32-40.* Looking at the lives of believers who suffered for Jesus answer the following questions.

1.  How did these people exercise their faith, even when they did not see God's promises fulfilled? (See Hebrews 11:1-2.)

2.  How did these people prove that they loved Jesus more than anything?

3.  Why does God say the world was not worthy of such people?

4.  What does it mean when it says "they might rise to a life far better" and "God provided something better for us?"

5.  Now read *Hebrews 12:1-2,* and summarize how these witnesses encourage us to run the race set before us, even if there is great difficulty.

## GOD WILL NOT ABANDON US

*Read Psalm 37:33-34.* God promised that He will not abandon us despite any trial we face. In Jesus, we are exalted to inherit a good land and a better heritage. Create a bookmark for your Bible with this Bible verse to remind you of God's faithfulness.

# DAILY DISCIPLESHIP

Here are a few tips as you read God's Word and use the journal pages to write down what you learn:

- What does the text say? Write down exact truths from the Bible.
- Let Scripture interpret Scripture. What do these verses mean? Be careful to not insert your own meaning into the text.
- How can you apply the truths of God's Word to your life? How should these truths change the way you think and live?

## DAY ONE

*Christ is our everything.*

- *Read Luke 14:25-27; Matthew 6:24; James 4:4; and 1 John 2:15*

Jesus is the Almighty God and the King of Kings. As the King, Jesus deserves all of our worship. We cannot worship halfway in when it comes to Christ. Either we love Jesus more than anything else, or we don't. We cannot be lukewarm. Charles Spurgeon said, "If Christ is not all to you, He is nothing to you."[3] That is not to say this isn't hard. Our hearts are prone to turn away from God. Still, we must remember and trust the gospel when we are tempted to place other people or desires above Jesus. Flee from loving the things of the world. Remember what Jesus did for you on the cross, and embrace Him as your Savior and Lord.

- What are some things that compete for Christ's rightful place of worship?

_____

_____

- Why is loving the things of the world wrong?

_____

_____

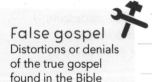

**False gospel**
Distortions or denials
of the true gospel
found in the Bible

_____

_____

## DAY TWO

*Jesus is better.*

- *Read Luke 14:27; John 12:24-25; Acts 20:24; Acts 21:13; and 2 Corinthians 12:10.*

The cross was a symbol of death. Yet Jesus uses this symbol to illustrate that we count our lives as insignificant compared to Him. If the Bible calls us to love our neighbor by sacrificing our popularity and sitting with the lonely kid, we do it because we love Jesus more than ourselves. If people spread lies about us or call us names for believing in Jesus, we endure and love those who are unkind to us because Jesus is better. Bearing your cross means choosing to be like Jesus. We should choose to do whatever it takes to look more like Jesus and obey His Word.

- If someone asked you what it meant to follow Christ, what would you say?

- Why is Paul content with weaknesses and hardships?

## DAY THREE

*We choose Jesus over everything.*

- *Read Luke 14:28-33; Philippians 3:8; Luke 9:25; and Matthew 8:19-22.*

In Luke 24:25, we see that great crowds were following Jesus. Many people were intrigued by Him, wanted to see miracles, wanted to be healed, or thought Jesus could be of some benefit to them. But how many stood by Him on His way to the cross? Zero. It's easy to follow Jesus when He looks like a miracle worker. It's a lot harder to follow Jesus when He leads you to suffering. Eventually, Jesus' resurrection opened the eyes of His disciples to what it truly means to follow Jesus, and they chose to renounce *(turn away)* everything for the sake of Jesus. In other words, as Paul said, we count everything as rubbish in order to love Christ with our all.

continued on next page >

● Why are some people drawn to Jesus at first, but then turn away?

● How can we think we are following Jesus, but really are not?

## DAY FOUR

*We sacrifice everything to gain an inheritance.*

● *Read Matthew 13:44-45; Matthew 19:21; 1 Corinthians 2:9; Luke 18:28-30; Matthew 6:33; and Mark 8:36.*

If you found billions of dollars hidden in a field, would you not sell everything you had to buy the field? What you own is probably no where near a billion dollars, so what you gain from losing all you have is more than you could imagine. This is similar to it is like with trusting in Jesus. By joyfully sacrificing all we have for Him, we gain infinitely more. In Jesus, we have an imperishable heritage secured for us in heaven, and the opposite is true as well. There is nothing we could gain in this world that compares to Christ. Everything that is Jesus' will be ours. In Him, we will be satisfied.

● What makes the things of this world so hard to let go of?

● How can we remember that Jesus is worth giving up everything?

## DAY FIVE

*Our suffering is not in vain.*

- *Read James 1:2-4, 12; Matthew 5:12; Romans 5:3-5; Hebrews 10:34-35; 1 Peter 4:13; and 2 Corinthians 4:17-18.*

Suffering is never easy, but suffering with joy takes bravery. It would be so easy to complain and whine about why we are going through a difficult time. Joy and suffering seem to be total opposites, but with God all things are possible. We find joy in knowing that our suffering is not in vain. Rather, it is producing a maturity of our faith and growing us to look more like Jesus. In fact, when we suffer with joy, we look more like Jesus, and people will take notice. Others will wonder how it is that a person can endure such struggles and still be joyful. Thus, it gives us an opportunity to share Jesus with others and tell them about the hope we have in Him. We can share how our present struggles are preparing for us an eternal glory that is beyond all compare.

- Why is suffering with joy important?

- How does suffering with joy prove that our faith is genuine?

## JOURNAL & PRAYER

# HOW DO I STUDY MY BIBLE?

### 1  STUDY ONE BIBLE BOOK

Who wrote the book?

When was the book written?

What is the book about?

What does the book say about God?

What people does the book tell about?

How did the people act toward God?

### 2  STUDY ONE BIBLE VERSE

Read the verse from different Bible translations.

What are the important words in the verse?

What are the words you don't understand?

Write the verse in your own words.

What can you learn from the verse?

### 3  STUDY ONE PERSON

When & where did the person live?

What took place in the person's life?

How did the person act?

What can you learn from the person?

# THE GOSPEL:
## GOD'S PLAN FOR ME

### GOD RULES

The Bible tells us God created everything, including you and me, and He is in charge of everything. Genesis 1:1; Revelation 4:11; Colossians 1:16-17

### WE SINNED

We all choose to disobey God. The Bible calls this sin. Sin separates us from God and deserves God's punishment of death. Romans 3:23; 6:23

### GOD PROVIDED

God sent Jesus, the perfect solution to our sin problem, to rescue us from the punishment we deserve. It's something we, as sinners, could never earn on our own. Jesus alone saves us. John 3:16; Ephesians 2:8-9

### JESUS GIVES

He lived a perfect life, died on the cross for our sins, and rose again. Because Jesus gave up His life for us, we can be welcomed into God's family for eternity. This is the best gift ever! Romans 5:8; 2 Corinthians 5:21; 1 Peter 3:18; Ephesians 2:8-9

### WE RESPOND

Believe in your heart that Jesus alone saves you through what He's already done on the cross. Repent, turning from self and sin to Jesus. Tell God and others that your faith is in Jesus. John 14:6; Romans 10:9-10, 13

# FAMILY GUIDES

Parents & families,

The following pages are here to help you extend each session conversation into the home. No one knows your preteen better than the you. We invite you into this special time as a way for you to disciple your preteens and help them grow in their faith.

—The Forged Team

# SESSION 1 FAMILY GUIDE

## WHO DEFINES TRUTH?

**Jesus is truth and determines what is true about His creation.** Truth is founded in the person of Jesus Christ. Who Jesus is and what He says is the foundation of all truth. Unlike the world's competing views of truth or the ever-changing truths found in culture, the truth founded in Jesus Christ does not change. His eternal nature and authority as Creator determine that truth is absolute. To know Jesus and to follow His words is to know truth.

Key Verse: *Romans 15:4*
Key Passages: *2 Timothy 3:16-17; Hebrews 1:1-2; Matthew 5:17-18*

## STUDY

What does the Bible say about who defines truth?
- The Bible affirms that truth is a Person—Jesus. As Creator, only Jesus holds the authority to declare what is true, and His eternal nature confirms that truth is absolute.

What does culture say about who defines truth?
- Culture often defines truth as relative—what's true for you may not be true for someone else. This belief is contradictory, as two opposing beliefs cannot both be true. (Example: Following Jesus and simply doing good works cannot both be the way to salvation.)

How does this change how you evaluate what is true in your own life?
- Having a relationship with Jesus and knowing God's Word help us to evaluate what is true and what is false so that we may live a life that is glorifying to God.

## DISCUSS

- Why should it matter to know and believe truth?

- The world is full of competing views on truth. If a friend tells you that he does not think that we can always know what is true about life, how would you respond?

- Do we simply choose to believe statements or ideas because they make us feel good or are popular? Or is there a standard by which we should measure what is true?

## PRAY

Take a few moments to pray over the concepts taught in this session. Thank God for sending His Son, Jesus, to reveal truth and for the truth of His Word. Confess any unbelief or sins that may be keeping you from believing Him. Ask God to help us value truth and discern what is true in order to bring Him glory.

## SEEK TRUTH SCAVENGER HUNT

- Create three different scavenger hunt directions for finding various objects hidden in your home. The first one should have missing words or phrases (e.g. "Walk ___ steps ___ ___ couch"). The second one should have words out of order or words used that do not make sense (e.g. "Go to the grass bed in the sandwich"). The third one should be the true scavenger hunt directions.

- Give preteens the directions listed in the order above. Allow some time for the frustration to set in before giving the final set of directions.

- Debrief as a family on how our world contains ideas that are completely untrue or may even contain partial truths, but they do not provide the complete truth. Discuss as a family how all truth originates from God and how we can turn to Him to find truth.

# SESSION 2 FAMILY GUIDE

## WHY SHOULD I TRUST THE BIBLE?

**The Bible is the trustworthy Word of God.** The words of the Bible are the very words of God given to us so we can know Him. Through the power of the Holy Spirit, God used men as the means by which His words were written. Over time, as God's Word was preserved, men recognized that the Scriptures were, in fact, divinely inspired. Through the measuring rod of a system called the canon, the Scriptures were organized into the Bible we have today. Additionally, Jesus affirmed and used the Scriptures to attest to the truth and reveal that all of Scripture points to Him.

*Key Verse: Romans 15:4*
*Key Passages: 2 Timothy 3:16-17; Hebrews 1:1-2; Matthew 5:17-18*

## STUDY

Who wrote the Bible?
- God Himself is the Divine Author of Scripture. Though the Bible was written by men, it is not the product of human creativity or human wisdom. The Bible is the very spoken, breathed-out words of the living God.

How did we get the Bible?
- From the days of Moses through the apostles of the New Testament, God's words were written and preserved by God's chosen divinely inspired authors. Over times, these words were recognized and measured by a standard of measures (the canon) as the very words of God. The Scriptures were organized into the Bible we have today.

Did Jesus affirm Scripture?
- Not only did Jesus affirm the words of God, but He also quoted the Scriptures. Jesus testified to the authority, truthfulness, and purpose of the Bible. (See Luke 24:27; Matt. 12:40; Matt. 4; and Mark 7:6-13.)

## DISCUSS

- Why is it important to believe God's Word is true and trustworthy?
- Why can I trust the different translations of the Bible? Are there any errors? (See Matt. 5:18; Matt. 24:35.)
- How did Jesus confirm the historical accuracy of the Bible? Were the people of the Bible actual people or just stories? (See Matt. 19:4-5; Matt. 8:11; and Matt. 24:15.)

## PRAY

Take a few moments to pray over the concepts taught in this session with your preteen. Give thanks to God for His Word and for providing us with a way to know Him. Ask God to help us to believe and live out the words of the Bible. Confess any unbelief or sin, asking God for forgiveness and the faith to believe He is trustworthy. Close with any prayer requests for your preteen.

## PROPHECIES FULFILLED

Look up the following Old Testament and New Testament verses, then discuss how the fulfillment of these prophecies provides evidence for the trustworthiness of the Bible.

- Genesis 3:15 and Galatians 4:4-5; Hebrews 2:14
- Genesis 12:3 and Galatians 3:8
- Genesis 14:18 and Hebrews 6:20
- Exodus 12:46 and John 19:31-36
- Numbers 21:9 and John 3:14-18; 12:32
- Isaiah 7:14 and Luke 1:35
- Isaiah 53:1 and John 18:1
- Daniel 9:26 and Matthew 27:50-51

There are many more fulfillments of the Old Testament found in Jesus that prove the trustworthiness of the Bible. What God promises will be done, and all of His words are true.

# SESSION 3 FAMILY GUIDE

## WHAT IS TRUE ABOUT GOD?

**The Bible tells us what is true about God's nature.** There is no one like our God. He is the maker of heaven and earth. He declares the end from the beginning. He has been, is, and will always be. He is the living God and the only God worthy of worship. God reveals what He is like through His attributes. Only God knows everything, and only God knows all that is true.

Key Verse: *Psalm 18:30*
Key Passage: *Isaiah 46:3-13*

## STUDY

Who is God?
- There is one God, but God exists eternally as three distinct, yet equal persons: the Father, the Son, and the Holy Spirit. God is an eternal being who is Spirit. (See John 4:24.) He is not limited to be in one place at one time (*omnipresence*). (See Ps. 139:7-10.) He is the living God and the only God worthy of worship. There is but one true God, and He has made Himself known to us!

What is God like?
- God has revealed what He is like through His attributes and the image of the invisible God, Jesus. His glory is displayed through His attributes such as His holiness, omniscience, omnipotence, goodness, and justice. By the truth of God's word and knowing Jesus, we grow in knowledge and love for God.

Does God really know everything?
- Only God knows everything, and only God knows all that is true. In Isaiah 46:10, we read of God's all-encompassing knowledge or what we refer to as "omniscience." God knows all things—past, present, future, what could be, etc. Therefore, we can trust Him without question. Add to this fact that God is truth, and we have every confidence to turn to Him for answers because we will always find what is true.

## DISCUSS

- How has God revealed Himself to us? (See Heb. 1:2-3 and 2 Tim. 3:16-17 for special revelation through His Word and Jesus; See Rom. 1:19-20 and Rom. 2:14-15 for general revelation through the creation.)
- Does God really know all truth? If so, how should the way you seek to know what is true change?
- Should growing in the truth about who God is affect our worship of Him? Why or why not?

## PRAY

Encourage your preteen to seek the truth about God through the daily devotionals provided in her Discipleship Guide. Pray that your preteen will grow in the knowledge of who God is and what He has done. Ask God to reveal Himself to her and make His presence known in her everyday life. Pray 3 John 1:4 over them: "I have no greater joy than this: to hear that my children are walking in truth."

## GOD'S ATTRIBUTES IN CREATION

Take a walk together through your neighborhood or a local park. Comment on all the beautiful things God has made. Discuss how what is created points to Him. We see His power in the warmth of the sun as it is upheld by His Word. We observe His creativity in the unusual bugs and creatures. We experience His goodness when we enjoy pleasant smells or pretty flowers. Ask questions to help your preteen think about all we can learn about God just from creation.

## WHAT DOES THE BIBLE SAY ABOUT ME?

**The Bible tells us what is true about ourselves.** All humans—male and female, every color and race—bear the image of God. All are created equally. All of humanity has intrinsic worth and value. Every life is valuable because our lives reflect the value and worthiness of God. Being made in the image of God also determines our purpose. Everything God does is for His glory. Therefore, as image bearers, everything we do should be for His glory as well. Unfortunately, the image we were created to reflect is broken because of sin, however, through the person and work of Jesus, God is restoring our broken image back to its perfect state. Jesus redeems our identity by making us a new creation. (See 2 Cor. 5:17.)

Key Verse: *Psalm 139:14*
Key Passages: *Genesis 1:26-31; Isaiah 43:7; Ephesians 2:1-10*

## STUDY

Who does God say I am?
- Our identity and who we are is bound to the truth that we are made in the image of God. In other words, God declares the truth of our identity by saying, "You are made to reflect me." God also states that as image bearers, we are all equal and valued by Him. Every life has intrinsic worth and value because we were created by an infinitely worthy God.

What is my purpose?
- God created all people to bring Him glory. As image bearers our purpose is to reflect God's glory to the world. If God does everything for His glory (See Is. 43:7), then we are also to mirror His mission. Glorifying God is not only what we are created to do, but it is also where we will find ultimate joy. (See John 15:11.) Did Jesus affirm Scripture?

Who am I in Christ?
- In Jesus, the broken image is being restored. Through faith in Jesus, God makes us into new creations who no longer desire to live according to the flesh. This renewed identity is given by God when we come to saving faith in Jesus. By growing in the truth, God renews our minds so that we look more like Jesus. Day by day, as we run to Jesus, the broken image is being restored.

## DISCUSS

- How can you as a family, as well as individually, look to Jesus more every day in your daily habits?

- How does the fact that people are created in the image of God change how you interact with each other? With your neighbors?

- How can you renew your mind to God's truth in order to become more like Jesus?

## PRAY

Give thanks to God for His saving grace and restorative work in your lives. Acknowledge Jesus' sacrifice so that you and your preteen can experience what it means to be a new creation. Confess any areas that might tempt you to steal God's glory for yourself or where you might treat another image bearer in an unloving way. Ask God to help you walk in His truth so that He may conform you into the image of Jesus.

## LOVE THY NEIGHBOR

All people bear the image of God. Therefore, everyone is valued and loved by Him. As a family, seek out a service project opportunity for a neighbor as a means to show they are loved. You could do yard work, make a meal, offer to watch their kids, and so forth. Even just a small gesture goes a long way to show you care.

# SESSION 5 FAMILY GUIDE

## WHAT DOES THE BIBLE SAY ABOUT THE CHURCH?

**The Bible tells us what is true about the church.** Jesus values the church. He is the head and we, the believers, are the body. One of Jesus' last commands to His disciples was to go build the church by making disciples. (See Matt. 28:19-20.) Being a part of a local body of believers is vital to our growth and is a means for us to glorify God. We bring glory to God by worshiping Him, edifying His people, and sharing the gospel with those who don't trust in Jesus.

Key Verse: *Hebrews 10:23*
Key Passages: *Ephesians 2:11-22; Acts 2:42-47; Ephesians 4:11-16*

## STUDY

Who is the church?
- The church is a regenerate people who have been reconciled with God by faith in Jesus. Being a part of a church identifies us with the household of God. We live in relationship with one another and with God, recognizing that Jesus is the head of the church. The church is made up of believers gathering together in a local setting in order to carry out the purposes God has ordained.

What is the purpose of the church?
- Ultimately, the purpose of the church is to glorify God. Within the church we have many ways we can bring glory to God. We worship God and teach truth to others. We sing praises to God. We gather together to encourage and pray for one another. We use our spiritual gifts to serve and bless others. We share the gospel and help our neighbor. In all these ways and more, God is glorified through our obedience to Him.

Why go to church?
- Being a part of a local body of believers is for our good. God desires that we grow in knowledge and become more

like Jesus (sanctification). The family of God is a living ministry that helps us to mature in our faith. Church shouldn't be viewed as an event we are obligated to attend. Rather, church should be a people we long to be in fellowship with, both for our good and God's glory.

## DISCUSS

- Why is it important to belong to a local church?
- How should we respond if we do not agree with another believer in the church? (This could be on a doctrinal issue, moral issue, etc.) How does this affect unity in the church?
- How can you as a family and individually serve your local church?

## PRAY

Ask your preteen if they have any specific prayers requests regarding church life. Maybe they are having a hard time making friends, or maybe they just don't know where they could serve. Pray over any requests they may have. Give thanks to God for the local church and the people He has brought into your life. Ask God to help you see how you can build up other believers into a mature faith and how you can be built up as well.

## SPIRITUAL GIFTS

Have you ever wondered what spiritual gifts God has given you? Spiritual gifts are a means to serve others and glorify God. Visit lifeway.com and enter the link below to learn more about spiritual gifts, and take an assessment to find out what your spiritual gift(s) might be. Remember to pray and ask God to help you know what gifts He has given you.

https://www.lifeway.com/en/articles/women-leadership-spiritual-gifts-growth-service

# SESSION 6 FAMILY GUIDE

## WHAT IS THE BIBLE ALL ABOUT?

**The Bible is God's message about Himself and His salvation plan through Jesus.** The Bible is the story of God. It provides us with truth about who God is, what He has done, and what He is doing. From Genesis to Revelation, we read of one narrative story where God is the Creator, Redeemer, and Restorer. Ultimately, the Bible points to Jesus as the One to whom and through whom all of God's story find its purpose. The Bible helps us know and be a part of what God is doing in and through His creation.

Key Verse: *Romans 3:23-24*
Key Passages: *Genesis 1:31; Genesis 3; Genesis 15; Romans 3:21-26; Acts 3:19-21; Revelation 21:1-5*

## STUDY

Where does the story start?
- The start of God's story in the world began at creation. God has eternally existed, but what was created had a beginning. The whole world and every living thing was created in six days. Everything God created was good and for God's glory. (See Isa. 43:7.) There was no sin, no death, no evil. God made a perfect world that was in perfect harmony with Him. However, sin entered God's good creation when Adam and Eve chose to disobey God's command. We call this part of the story *the fall*.

What has God done in the story?
- After Adam and Eve sinned, death and wickedness entered the world. God's good creation was broken. But God had a plan. God would send a Savior to redeem the broken and sinful creation. In Genesis 3:15, we read the first promise God made to send Jesus into the world! Jesus is the only hope for a sinful world. Apart from Him, there would be no redemption.

Where is the story headed?
- God's story isn't finished. He has done great things, but He is still working to make things new. We call this restoration. God is restoring what was lost and broken. Restoring doesn't just mean that we will go back to the way things were in Eden before the fall. God's act of restoration is leading the story to something even better. There will be a new heaven and a new earth where we will dwell with God forever.

## DISCUSS

- Why is knowing the Bible's big story important for our faith? What hope does it give us?

- Why is it important to read and know the smaller stories of the Bible? How do they remind us God is faithful? How do they point us to Jesus?

- What acts of redemption and restoration has God done in your own life?

## PRAY

Take a few moments as a family to thank God for the acts of redemption and restoration He has already done in your own lives and in the world around us. Ask God to help you trust in Him as He finishes the story He began. Ask Him to lead you in truth, running to Jesus— the author and perfecter of your faith.

## THE BIG PICTURE GOSPEL STORY

Pretend you are sharing the gospel with an unbeliever. Practice sharing the gospel using the four parts of the Biblical narrative: creation, fall, redemption, restoration.

## IS THE BIBLE MORE IMPORTANT THAN OTHER BOOKS?

**The Bible is holy and different than sacred texts of other religions and worldviews.** There are many different religious books and worldviews, all with competing claims on truth. The Bible is the only book that is the authoritative Word of God and leads us in all truth. It is a book which is living and active, and it changes lives. The Bible proves itself true by fulfilled prophecies, eyewitness testimonies, numerous copies of ancient manuscripts, and the power to transform lives.

Key Verse: *2 Timothy 3:16-17*
Key Passage: *1 Corinthians 15:1-11*

## STUDY

How is the Bible different from other books?
- Paul references the fulfilled prophecies of the Bible as evidence for the resurrection. Unlike other religious books, the Bible proves itself true by fulfilling what was written long before the event ever happened. No other religious book has ever predicted an event and seen it come true. Only a book written by an all-knowing, all-powerful God could predict future events. Additionally, the number of ancient copies of the Scriptures verifies its reliability and trustworthiness.

What other evidence proves the Bible is more important?
- What is written in the Scriptures was actually seen. When Jesus rose from the dead, He appeared to Peter, then to the rest of the disciples, then to over 500 people at once, then to James, then the rest of the apostles. Anyone knows that the more witnesses you have to an event, the more you can prove the event really is true. The four authors of the gospel were also eyewitnesses to the life, miracles, death and resurrection of Jesus as well.

What makes the Bible holy and special?
- Paul's life was changed when He met Jesus on the road to Damascus. His conversion is an extremely credible witness. How else could you explain going from hating Jesus to being willing to die for Jesus? Not only that, but the other apostles also risked their lives for the sake of the gospel. Many even died while trying to take the good news of Jesus to the world. The Bible is the most important book because it has the power to transform lives.

## DISCUSS

- How do I know the Bible is true and other religious books are not?
- How do I interact with people who disagree with the Bible?
- How do I love people who reject the Bible/Jesus?

## PRAY

Talk with your preteen about any questions or doubts they may have about the Bible. Remind them that God is big enough to handle any questions they have, and that His Word is sufficient to answer them. Pray over any prayer requests or concerns. Ask God to make His Word a source of comfort and power in your life. Thank God for the gift of the Bible and for how it has the power to change lives.

## TRANSFORMATIONAL POWER OF GOD'S WORD

Parents take the opportunity to share with your preteen how the Bible has changed your life. Perhaps you may even know of someone in your church that might be willing to share their story as well. Help your preteen to recognize that the Bible is the Word of God and is the most important book they will ever read.

# SESSION 8 FAMILY GUIDE

## WHY SHOULD I CARE WHAT THE BIBLE SAYS?

**The Bible leads us to walk in a manner pleasing to God.** The Bible helps us renew our minds so that we are able to walk in the Spirit and not the flesh. Because God changes our hearts when we trust in Him, we no longer want to live as the world lives. Rather, we want our lives to reflect a holy God whose grace has saved us from our sins. The Bible helps us to grow in relationship with God, renew our minds, and become more like Jesus through sanctification.

Key Verse: *Matthew 4:4*
Key Passage: *Ephesians 4:17-32*

## STUDY

How does the Bible grow our relationship with God?

- God gave us the Bible to establish and grow our relationship with Him. Paul gave the church at Ephesus a contrast between unbelieving Gentiles and Christians. The Gentiles' minds were darkened by sin and alienated from God. In other words, because of their unbelief, they did not have a relationship with God. They were still separated from Him because of their sin. On the other hand, Paul said that those who are in relationship with God came to faith because they were taught in the truth of Jesus—from God's Word!

How does the Bible renew our minds?

- To be renewed is to have a total transformation of the whole person. The only way to be renewed in how we think is to continually look to Jesus. After all, Jesus is the image we are being made into. (See Rom. 8:29.) Where do we go to know Jesus more and more? Our Bible! It is the truth of God's Word that renews our minds. As we read God's Word, the Holy Spirit works in our hearts and minds to help us look more like Jesus. (See 2 Cor. 3:18.)

What does the new self look like?

- God is working in us to transform us more into the image of Jesus. We call this process sanctification. The more we look to Jesus by studying God's Word, the more God changes us to look like Jesus. The process of sanctification is not always easy. While God does the work, we must be obedient to renew our minds. As we abide in Jesus, our lives will bear fruit that shows are faith is genuine. God will be faithful to finish the good work He began in us. (See Phil. 1:6.)

## DISCUSS

- How do I study the Bible in order to renew my mind?

- How does grace work when I fail to live up to God's standard of holiness?

- Why does it matter that my life is set apart by holiness?

## PRAY

Ask your preteen to share any concerns or prayer requests. Thank God for the gift of His Word and the grace of Jesus that covers all our sin. Pray for God to renew your minds and continue to sanctify you in His truth. Ask God to help you walk in holiness, reflecting His glory to the world.

## BIBLE READING PLAN

Our hearts should desire to read God's Word in order to know God more and grow more into the image of Jesus. Perhaps as a family you could develop your own Bible reading plan. You could choose to read through a book of the Bible in a month or read through the whole Bible in one year. Whatever option you choose, reading God's Word should be a priority for every believer.

# SESSION 9 FAMILY GUIDE

## DOES THE BIBLE TELL ME ALL I NEED TO KNOW?

**The Bible tells us that Jesus supplies our every need.** All of Scripture points to Jesus as the all-satisfying and essential need of every person. Not only is He our Savior and King, but He also provides us with everything we need to live a godly life this side of eternity. In Jesus, we find the hope, wisdom, and grace to traverse every part of life. While we often strive to "be good" and sometimes believe we need to earn favor with God, the Bible shows us that a perfect life is impossible. We all struggle with idols of the heart, and we all will fail to live up to God's standard of holiness. However, in Jesus it is possible to not only find eternal life, but also be given the grace to live a godly life for His glory.

Key Verse: *2 Peter 1:3*
Key Passage: *Matthew 19:16-26*

## STUDY

Are we good enough?
- At times we can all struggle with wanting to earn favor. Even the rich young ruler wanted to know how he could earn eternal life and favor with God. In fact, many believe that salvation is earned by how good we are or how we're not as bad as others. Yet Jesus plainly tells the rich young ruler that no one but God is good. No one can keep all of the commandments because only God is perfectly holy..

How does the Law reveal our shortcomings?
- The rich young ruler believed he had kept the law. However, a task given by Jesus quickly reveals that this young ruler had an idol of the heart—his wealth. It may be easy to judge this man, but how often do we fail to love God more than other things? The Bible helps us recognize our shortcomings and reveals our own idols. We also see that these idols will never satisfy our hearts. Only Jesus can do that!

Who then can be saved?
- Jesus' disciples understood that, according to God's standards, it would be impossible for anyone to be saved. However, Jesus brings good news! While it would be impossible for us to earn salvation, all things are possible with God. Jesus does what we cannot do. Jesus lived a sinless life and died on the cross to take the punishment we deserve for our sin. Jesus' death and resurrection made it possible for us to be counted as righteous and have a relationship with God when we trust in Him. The impossible becomes possible through Jesus! Jesus also helps us to live a godly life now by His grace.

## DISCUSS

- What are ways you struggle to earn God's favor?
- How does Jesus help me when I fail to live up to God's standards?
- How does God's grace help me live a godly life now? What if the Bible doesn't address a specific situation where I may struggle?

## PRAY

Ask your preteen to join you in a time of prayer. Thank God for His free gift of salvation that cannot be earned. Ask the Lord to move in your preteen's heart to flee from worldly standards and run to the grace of Jesus. Allow your preteen to share any prayer requests, especially in regards to how they may need Jesus' grace in specific struggles.

## FAMILY QUESTION BOX

God's Word tells us that Jesus will supply all of our needs. In today's culture, we sometimes come across situations that are difficult to navigate or leave us asking questions. Create a question box that you place in your home where your preteen can drop in questions she may have regarding faith and everyday living. Determine a time for you all to sit down and answer the questions together using God's Word.

## IS HEAVEN REAL?

**The Bible tells us what is true about eternal life.** Our life on this earth is a vapor. (See Jas. 4:14.) While this may sound dismal, for the believer, it is a glorious truth. Not only is heaven real, but it is the place where God most fully reveals His glory. We were made to be with God, and heaven is the place where that truth will become a reality for everyone who trusts in Jesus for salvation. Heaven will be the most beautiful, glorious, all-satisfying place that we have ever known or will know. When we die, anyone who is in Christ will immediately be reunited with Him in heaven. One day, God will create a new heaven and earth where He will dwell with us forever.

Key Verse: *Philippians 3:20-21*
Key Passages: *John 6:38-42;*
*2 Corinthians 5:1-10; Revelation 21:9-27*

## STUDY

Is heaven an actual place?
- In these verses, Jesus not only testifies that heaven is an actual place, but He also tells us that God desires we live there with Him. God promises that Jesus' life, death, and resurrection would secure eternal life for all who believe in Him. Heaven is a place where followers of Jesus will live. For those who place their faith in Christ, heaven will be the home they have always longed for because being with God is our heart's greatest longing.

What happens when we die?
- God does not leave followers of Jesus to wonder what will happen to us after we die. He promises us an eternal dwelling place immediately after death. To be here on earth is to be away from God, but when we depart this earth we instantly go to heaven. Sadly, not everyone will go to heaven. While God desires that all repent and trust in Jesus for salvation (1 Tim. 2:4), there are many people who will reject Jesus. We can be

a part of God's mission by telling other people about Jesus.

What is eternity like?
- One day, God will create the new heavens and the new earth. As such, God's space (heaven) will be joined to our space (earth) to build an everlasting home. We see in these verses that the new heaven and earth will be a city. It is a very physical space where God will dwell with His people forever. In this city will be people from every nation, tribe, and tongue—all worshiping God and enjoying Him forever. Our hearts will eternally be satisfied by Jesus and we will experience His goodness forever.

## DISCUSS

- What is true about heaven that you didn't know or had misconceptions about?

- How does how you live now affect your eternity?

- Why will Jesus' presence make heaven better than anything else?

## PRAY

Discuss any questions your preteen may have about heaven or eternity. Pray that God's Word may bring peace and hope, knowing that those who believe in Jesus have a home awaiting them. Ask God to help keep your minds fixed on heavenly things, that you might live for God's kingdom, knowing what is here is perishable. Thank God for the hope we have in Jesus and that because of Him we will one day live with God.

## ENCOURAGE ONE ANOTHER

1 Thessalonians 4:13-18 describes the second coming of Christ. At the end of the passage, Paul gives the exhortation to encourage one another with these words. As a family, read these verses together and think about how they are encouraging. Discuss ways as a family you can encourage each other through scripture to look forward to heaven and Christ's return.

## WILL GOD REALLY JUDGE ME?

**The Bible tells us what is true about judgment.** One day all people will stand to give an account of their lives before God. In His mercy, God sent Jesus to take the full punishment for our sin and plead guilty on our behalf. Those who are in Christ Jesus will find that every sin has been forgiven forever. Still, how we live matters. Will we show our faith to be genuine by how we love God and others, or will we live how we want without regard to Jesus' commands?

Key Verse: *Numbers 14:18*
Key Passages: *Luke 16:19-31; Revelation 20:11-15*

## STUDY

Why do faith and right actions matter?
- Jesus tells the story of the rich man and Lazarus to help us understand that how we live our life matters. We cannot expect to live only for ourselves, doing what pleases us without regard to God's commands. Jesus said that the greatest commandments are to love God and love others. (See Matt.22:38-39.) Our right actions do not save us, but they are the evidence of a life of faith. God sees our good deeds and recognizes them as the fruits or evidence of our faith.

Is God's judgment really just?
- One attribute or character trait of God that seems to make people uneasy or upset is that God is just. Common questions about God and justice are, "Isn't God all-loving? How can He send people to hell?" The problem with this idea of thinking is that we believe we do not deserve God's punishment for our sin. This couldn't be further from the truth. Every single person is deserving of God's just punishment for sin. God's holiness cannot let sinful, unrepentant people enter heaven, and God's justice gives just punishment. But that's not all! God's holiness and justice has also provided a way for us to be forgiven and found not guilty! In Jesus, all of our sin is forgiven and His righteousness is placed on us.

What will the final judgment be like?
- God does not desire that anyone should be separated from Him, but His mercy and grace will not last forever. Eventually, judgment will come to us all, and this judgment only has two outcomes: live with Christ forever, or be separated from Him forever. At the final judgment, books will be opened. Several books will contain what we have done (*our actions*). One book will contain the book of life. In this book are written the names of everyone who has repented and turned to Jesus for salvation. Because of Jesus, Christians will experience God's loving kindness, grace, and mercy with Him forever.

## DISCUSS

- What does it mean to reject God/Jesus?
- How does Jesus' sacrifice for our sins satisfy the wrath of God?
- Why should Christians look forward to Christ's return and judgment?

## PRAY

Pray over your preteen asking God to help him to know the love of God. Ask God to help your preteen bear fruits of their faith and show a lost world the love of Christ. Thank God for His Son, Jesus, who will judge us according to His righteousness and find us not guilty.

## SPIRITUAL GIFTS

Eschatology is a fancy word for the study of the end times. Right now we live in the tension of the "already but not yet." Christ has come once, but He has not yet come back. He will come again. As a family, study the verses listed to see how the Bible describes the end times. Discuss how we can find hope in knowing Jesus is coming again.
- Joel 2:28-3;, 2 Timothy 3:1-5; Matthew 24:1-51; 2 Peter 3:10-13; 2 Thessalonians 2:3-4; Revelation 20–22

# SESSION 12 FAMILY GUIDE

## HOW CAN I BE USED BY GOD?

**The Bible tells us what is true about God's mission for us.** It's pretty amazing that the God of all creation has a job for us! What could be more exciting than joining God on His mission and being used to bring Him glory? No matter who we are, God desires that every follower of Jesus be on mission with Him. God wants to use each of us to share the good news of Jesus Christ. Every person is unique in the ways God can use him. Some of us will take the gospel to far places of the world and some of us will lead our next door neighbor to Christ. As Christians, we have the best news that ever existed! Though being on mission with God may sometimes be scary or cause people to mock us, we are called to trust Him and be obedient to His calling. Just as Jesus loved lost people, so should we show our love for all people by sharing the gospel.

Key Verse: *Romans 10:14-15*
Key Passage: *Acts 17:16-34*

## STUDY

Do I have a heart for the lost?
- God has a heart for the lost. Our heart should find compassion and even grief over those who do not know Jesus. Just as Paul took the gospel to all different people, so should we share Jesus with others. Jesus invites us to be a part of His work and has given us everything we need in His Word to share this truth with others. We have the joy of being called a laborer for Christ, and He's calling us to help Him reap a harvest of people who love and trust Him for His glory.

How do I know what to say?
- Paul was a student of God's Word. He knew the Scriptures and believed that all of God's Word was truth. In these verses, Paul quoted Old Testament passages in order to persuade the men of Athens to believe in the one true God. It is important to know the words of truth in order to speak truth to others. Being in the Word gives us the confidence, the power, and the knowledge to share the gospel with others. While we should be a student of the Word, God does not expect us to know everything. But we do have the answer to salvation—Jesus! We can begin sharing our faith by telling others about Jesus.

What if people mock me?
- God does not promise us that being on mission with Him will always go smoothly. There will be many times when people may laugh at you or make fun of you for your faith—even Paul had people who mocked him when he shared Christ. Yet we do not let people's reactions interfere with our obedience. We don't always know how the listener will respond, but we can be obedient to share the gospel with all who will hear. God will do the hard work of changing hearts.

## DISCUSS

- Why is it important that I share the gospel with others?
- How can I overcome my fear of sharing the gospel?
- Who in my life needs to hear the good news of the gospel?

## PRAY

Take a few moments to pray with your preteen. Ask God to help you be on mission for Him. Ask God to give you the boldness and the obedience to faithfully share His Word with others. Thank God for His promise to help us in times of need and be with us always. Ask God to use you for His glory.

## MISSIONARY CARDS

- Collect missionary index cards from your church. (If you do not have any, use the IMB website to print off missionaries you can pray for. (https://www.imb.org/pray/)
- Using an index card ring, create a booklet of the different cards.
- Commit to praying for these missionaries.

## HOW DO I KEEP FOLLOWING JESUS WHEN THINGS ARE DIFFICULT?

**The Bible tells us what is true about following Jesus.** There are some people who think that following Jesus means a life of ease and comfort. They believe that Jesus will grant them their hearts' desires because they have called Him 'Lord,' but this is a false gospel. Jesus never promised us that life would be easy and give us worldly comforts. When we come to saving faith in Jesus, our lives do get better. We find joy, peace, and hope knowing that in Jesus, we have new life. However, this does not necessarily mean that all of our problems go away. In fact, the circumstances of our lives may get worse. Jesus told His disciples that they would face trials. He called them to count the cost of following Him. As believers, we too have to count the cost of following Jesus because at some point, we will have to ask ourselves if Jesus is worth it.

**Key Verse:** *Philippians 3:8*
**Key Passages:** *Luke 14:25-33; Matthew 13:44-45; James 1:2-4,12*

## STUDY

Do I love Jesus more than anything?
- The words Jesus spoke in these verses may be hard to hear. They definitely would have shocked the people He was talking to. We know from His other teachings and the rest of the Bible's testimony that God does not want us to hate people. It is likely that Jesus used such strong language to get people's attention, but then help them see that for Him to have the proper place in their lives, every other relationship must seem like hate in comparison for their love for Him. How will we respond when Jesus says, "Follow me"?

What will it cost me to follow Jesus?
- Something that every believer must be willing to consider is what it will cost to follow Jesus. Jesus described counting the cost as adding up all the money it would take to construct a building, or if going to war would be worth the sacrifice of the king's men, especially if he loses the war. Likewise, we must consider the cost. In verse 33, Jesus said that following Him could cost everything. Thousands of believers have suffered, lost their possessions,

and given their lives because they loved Jesus more than anything in this world.

Is Jesus worth the cost?
- Jesus told these parables to remind us that despite what we lose on this earth, what we gain following Jesus will be far greater. We count the cost and joyfully sacrifice because we gain Christ. He is our reward. He is our joy. And not only do we gain Jesus, but we gain everything along with Him. We have an imperishable inheritance awaiting us in heaven. (See 1 Peter 1:4.) James tells us to count the trials of our faith as joy. When we face trials—and we will—we should do so with joy, knowing that Jesus is worth it. We are joyful because we know trials are a means for God to grow us more into the image of His Son.

## DISCUSS

- Why should I choose to follow Jesus no matter how much it costs?
- What are some of God's promises to help me endure trials?
- How can I be joyful in suffering?

## PRAY

Ask your preteen if she has any prayer requests. Go before God in prayer and thank God for His promises of faithfulness and unfailing love during difficult times. Ask God to help you to trust in Him and persevere through trials. Ask God to give you joy when difficulties arise. Praise Him for the reward we are promised despite whatever we lose on this earth.

## SUFFERERS FOR CHRIST

As a family, choose to read a biography on a Christian who counted it joy to suffer for Christ. Oftentimes the testimonies of others encourage us to stand firm in our faith and endure trials. There are many who have willingly given all that they would gain Jesus. Here is a list to consider as you get started:

- Dietrich Bonhoeffer
- Jim Elliot
- Corrie Ten Boom
- Amy Carmichael
- Adoniram Judson/Ann Judson

# GLOSSARY OF KEY TERMS

**Atonement (n.):** The work of Jesus to cover or cancel sin; Jesus made atonement for our sins when He died on the cross. (Heb. 2:17)

**Attribute of God (n.):** A quality or feature describing the character of God

**Worldview (n.):** How we view the world—our basic beliefs about God, humanity, ethics, the world around us

**Canon (n.):** The list of all the books that belong in the Bible

**Church (n.):** A group of believers who meet together to worship and serve God

**Covenant relationship (n.):** A mutual agreement between two people or groups of people. The covenant between God and people is unique because God alone sets the conditions.

**Culture (n.):** The set of shared attitudes, values, goals, and practices that characterizes a group of people

**Doctrine (n.):** What the whole Bible teaches us today about a particular topic

**Eyewitness Testimony (n.):** Witness to an event, someone who has seen something with their own eyes and shares their experience

**The Fall (n.):** The coming of sin into the world

**False Gospel (n.):** Distortions or denials of the true gospel found in the Bible

**God's Holiness (n.):** The intrinsic worth, beauty, purity, value, and excellence of God; God is above all else, nothing is like Him

**God's mission (n.):** The plan and purpose of God among us to glorify Himself through the work of redeeming people and restoring His creation

**Gospel (n.):** The truth about who Jesus is *(the Son of God/fully God and fully man)* and what He did *(lived a perfect life, died on the cross for our sins, and rose again)*

**Heaven (n.):** A real place where God most fully reveals His glory, and where angels, other heavenly creatures, and redeemed Christians all worship Him

**Truth (n.):** Who God is and what He says

**Identity (n.):** Who a person is in relation to what God says is true about them

**Inerrant (adj.):** The truth that Scripture in its original form does not contain anything contrary to fact

**Infallible (adj.):** Free of error, the truth that Scripture is not able to lead us astray in faith and practice

**Inspiration (n.):** God-breathed, the truth that God inspired people to write the Scriptures

**Justification (n.):** The truth that when God says that our sins are forgiven, we are made righteous

**Lost (adj.):** Term used in the Bible to refer to people who have not trusted in Jesus as Lord and Savior

**New Heavens and New Earth (n.):** The entirely renewed creation where believers will dwell with God forever; one day Jesus will return and make all things new.

**Omnipotence (n.):** God's unlimited power and authority

**Omniscience (n.):** God's complete knowledge of Himself and all things— all past, present, and future events, both actual and possible

**Rationalize (v.):** Attempting to explain or justify your behavior with logical reasons, even if they are not true

**Reconcile (v.):** The removal of iniquity and restoration between God and people (See Matthew 5:24; Romans 5:10.)

**Redemption (n.):** God's work to release believers from the consequences of sin when they trust in Jesus (See Rom. 3:24; Eph. 1:7.)

**Regenerate (v.):** To be born again, made a new creation; spiritually speaking, this term reflects what happens when a person becomes a Christian (See John 1:13; 1 Peter 1:23; Titus 3:5.)

**Renewed (adj.):** Completely transformed

**Restoration (n.):** The truth that God is making all things new (Rev. 21:5)

**Sanctification (n.):** The process of becoming more like Jesus by the power of the Holy Spirit

**Sin (v.):** To think, say, or behave in any way that goes against God and His commands

**Sovereignty (n.):** God's power and control over His creation

**Theology (n.):** The study of God and the pursuit of knowing God

**Transformation (n.):** Changed outwardly or inwardly; (See Rom. 12:2; 2 Cor. 3:18.) in the Bible, transformation often results from an encounter with God in Christ

**Works (n.):** Right actions that give evidence of genuine faith and transformation that has occurred in the life of a believer

# END NOTES

1.  CS Lewis, *The Problem of Pain*. (New York: Macmillan, 1944).

2.  Randy Alcorn, *50 Days of Heaven*. (Illinois: Tyndale House, 2006).

3.  Charles Spurgeon, "Christ Is All." Sermon, Metropolitan Tabernacle, Newington, CT, August 20, 1871.